May 4th 1926.

Henry Moore.

38 Grove Studios
Adie Road
Hammersmith

Development

√ Sculpture from now.
not back to Maillol
+ archaic Greek.

SCULPTURE + modelling

Disposition of masses + exposition

Theories   exposition

Define difference between modelled & sculpture
+ Keep in mind —

Sculpture in relation to mass
modelling is creation

Write not Theories of art

what I am attempting to do

connection with my own life — + vision.
make notes each night of something observed during day

Keep ever prominent the big view of sculpture
The World Tradition

Portrait of an Artist

HENRY MOORE

by
John Read

Whizzard Press/André Deutsch

Published by Whizzard Press
in association with André Deutsch Ltd., 1979
105 Great Russell Street London W.C.1.

ISBN 0 233 97174 2

Colour separation by Printing House Reproduction Ltd.
Typesetting by South Bucks Typesetters Ltd.
Made and printed in Great Britain by Waterlow Ltd, Dunstable.

CONTENTS

AUTHOR'S NOTE

I would like to thank the British Broadcasting Corporation for permission to make use of statements by Henry Moore contained in various films produced by the author between 1951 and 1978.

I am particularly grateful to Mr David Mitchinson and the staff of the Henry Moore Foundation for their patient and painstaking assistance in helping me to prepare material for inclusion in this book; and I would especially like to thank Henry Moore himself for so generously giving of his time, both now and over the years, to enable me to write so directly about his life and his work.

Finally, my thanks to Louise for helping to prepare the manuscript, and to Lucy for typing it so promptly and efficiently.

CHAPTER ONE
PROFILE

By his 80th birthday, Henry Moore, Order of Merit, Companion of Honour, had received at least 75 major awards in the form of honorary degrees, memberships of Art Academies in several countries, and international prizes for art. He had held 70 exhibitions of his work in at least 25 different countries. He was the originator of some 800 sculptures, great and small, and more than 4,000 drawings and sketches; and his more recent interest in graphics has already yielded some 500 prints of various kinds. Major collections of his work are owned by public galleries in London, Toronto and New York, and there is hardly a museum of modern art of importance in Europe, U.S.A. or Japan which does not own at least an example of his sculptures. Complete sets of his graphic work have been given to museums in London, Paris, Duisberg and Toronto. Few artists in the 20th century have achieved such world-wide fame or been so generous in their support of public collections. No sculptor in history has had his work so widely shown around the world. Only the Soviet Union and China have so far ignored his art, a sharp reminder of the effectiveness of the cultural and political barriers which still persist in an age of international communication.

Such eminence and fame invites cynicism and indeed jealousy. Moore has been called "the last of the Romantics" by those who assume that Romanticism, whatever that may be, has run its course. He has been accused of unfairly overshadowing the young, of producing sculpture to order for the prestige of wealthy clients and of being no more than a fortunate beneficiary of the international gallery system—and a product of their promotion and salesmanship. To others, at the beginning of his career, he was a corrupter of youth—a Bolshevik—a man who had "been feeding on garbage", who wilfully mutilated and distorted the human figure for reasons best known to himself. In England he was continuously looked upon as a leader of the *avant-garde*, the man who made sculptures with holes in the middle and had become a symbol for "modern art". Though he was at a certain period in his life bitterly attacked by members of the British Royal Academy, he is now regarded as something of an institution himself.

As a film-maker I have known Henry Moore, on and off, for thirty years. I find it exceedingly difficult to recognize either the artist or the man in some of the criticisms that have inevitably been made. Thirty

Henry Moore: the hands
of a sculptor.

'Hoglands'—Henry Moore's home for the past
40 years. To begin with there was just one small
studio; now there are nine studios, the archives,
and a resident community of helpers.

years ago, in 1950, he was living in a 17th-century farmhouse in the
hamlet of Perry Green, in Hertfordshire, which he had bought during the
Second World War. He still lives there. The house cost £900 and he
could just afford the £300 deposit because he had sold a large elm wood
reclining figure, which he had completed in 1939. It represented the
climax of his development before the war. Its sale enabled Moore to buy
for the first time a proper place to live and work. He was then 41 years
old.

In 1950 Moore's studio was still confined to the small building adjoining
the house. It was hardly bigger than a garage and one end of it had once
been the village shop. Now he has nine studios standing in over forty
acres of grounds. The largest of these stands at the bottom of a flat expanse of parkland surrounded by hedges, fields and trees, and planted
with willows. Sculptures are displayed in carefully arranged positions
against the landscape or the sky. The big studio is a huge transparent
construction rather like a greenhouse and about 50 feet (15·2 m) high.
From time to time, a massive mobile crane comes to dip inside and
delicately extract sections of his full scale maquettes, bringing them to rest
on a 30 ton lorry that is waiting to take the pieces to the bronze foundry.
Sometimes these sculptures are as much as 20 feet (6·1 m) in length and

The largest of Moore's nine studios.
From here the full-scale maquettes are
transported to the bronze foundry.

rise 15 feet (4·7 m) high. The first sculpture that Moore sold cost its purchaser £5. You could hold it in your hand. Now the largest can cost more than £100,000 to make, and may sell for three times that amount.

The other buildings lie adjacent to this big "glasshouse". One has a raised platform outside its sliding doors so that sculptures can be wheeled out into the sun and air. Another contains a place where Moore can sit and draw by the window, or work on the plaster models which develop out of the original hand-sized maquettes he makes for each new idea. Off this room is another lined with shelves painted white and brightly lit by skylights. It is a mass of detail. The shelves are packed with objects of every kind—model sculptures or parts of them, bones, flints, pieces of weathered wood or root. Hundreds more lie in boxes, on tables, among a litter of tools, tins, bottles, jars and bags of plaster. In this bric-a-brac an eye familiar with Moore's sculptures can often find something that was the starting-point for one of his works. It is here, sitting in a battered wicker-work chair and wearing a butcher's apron, that he scrapes away at the hard plaster-shape in his hand with a penknife, gradually giving to it a form which already exists in his mind's eye.

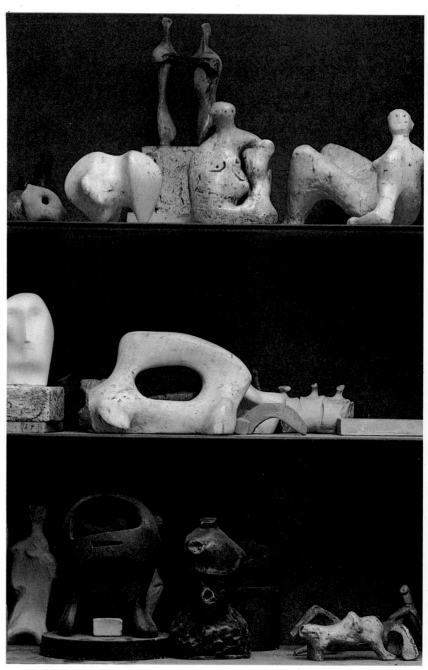

Various objects in the maquette studio.

The fourth studio is sometimes used for storage or for carving his wooden figures. It has been painted inside with vague cloud forms sprayed on the walls and can be used to photograph larger works. Fields stretch around as far as the eye can see. One leads into a small wood and sometimes several of his full-scale plaster models can be found there, covered in lichen or dead leaves. A larger field spreads to a gentle hill on the horizon. This hill was carefully built up by bulldozers to Moore's own design. It provides a viewpoint over miles of countryside and he likes to place sculptures on it to judge their effect from a distance. Beyond, a path leads to a gravel-pit that forms a small lake. It is a peaceful place to walk and Moore intends to put a sculpture there, arising from the water.

Returning to the house, you pass through an apple orchard. To one side, rather lost beyond a hedge and a vegetable garden, is a hut which is now neatly fitted out with shelves, screens and cupboards. It is the only work place with a carpet and Moore uses it as his graphic studio. In a corner by the window there is a small desk and a rough chair with two pieces of foam rubber as cushions. Above the desk the wall is covered with postcards, hastily written notes, and photographs and illustrations. You might find a reproduction of a drawing by Rembrandt or Dürer or

Master etcher Jacques Frélaut (who also worked with Picasso) with Henry Moore.

Degas pinned next to an invitation to an exhibition. It is his favourite place for sketching. Nearby is another shed equipped with camera and tripod, where Moore likes to photograph his smaller sculptures.

Beyond the house, the original studio is still in use, mainly as a place to store smaller works that have come back from the bronze foundry to be polished and fitted to their bases by his assistants. In a backroom there is a printing-press. This is where Moore works on etchings and aquatints. It has the feeling of a private retreat.

The last building is a new acquisition. A simple brick house has been converted and extended to form the premises of the Henry Moore Foundation. All the archives are now there. There is a strong-room, and a long, tall carving studio. There are also three floors of open-plan offices and work spaces that look out onto a huge conservatory and reception area, from which one can see a great expanse of landscape and sky. There is not a sculpture in sight. His secretary and a staff of four attend to the daily events of Moore's life and the massive archives of drawings, prints and literature that relate to his work. There are five incoming telephone lines, and a small exchange connects with the house and the nine studios. Looking from the village green opposite, at the high gabled white-fronted house, the neat lawn and the trim fence with its willow trees and shrubs, it is difficult to believe that anything unusual goes on beyond this peaceful rural facade.

Across the green lie some once derelict farm buildings. Moore's two part-time sculptor assistants, Malcolm Woodward and Michel Muller, live in the cottages. David Mitchinson, who has worked on the Henry Moore collection for eleven years, has a house behind the inn. The old barn is packed inside, not with hay or animal feed, but with piles of sturdy wooden crates covered in stencilled lettering and labels from all over the world—New York, Jerusalem, Tokyo, Hamburg, Amsterdam, Florence, and so on. Inside the crates, looking like caged animals, a huge stock of sculptures lie in wait for the next exhibition, wherever in the world that may be.

Nowadays nearly half the village is occupied or used by this ever-growing sculptural community. In spite of this great expansion in Moore's activities, at first sight little seems to have changed in the thirty years that I have known the place. Betty Tinsley has always lived in the village and is still Moore's secretary. She still addresses him as "Mr Moore". Frank Farnham, a local builder who lives next door but one, still busies himself, supervising the handling of the sculptures, the running of the studios, and the construction of rostra, plinths, crates and turntables. Frank's son John has spent his life around the studios, helping his father, learning the techniques, and assisting with the polishing and patinating of the sculptures. He has become a sculptor himself. Moore's daughter, Mary, has grown up, married, and lives nearby—Moore has now a grandson and a new subject for his sketchbook. His wife, Irina, still prepares the one o'clock lunch and expects punctuality. As the estate has grown, she has attended to an ever-expanding garden, planting willow trees, collecting cacti and tending the bushes and flowers. Her presence brings an essential order to the life of a busy and impulsive man, who can change his mind without warning and who revels in keeping everything on the go at the same time.

Moore's house remains what it always was, a warm, domestic home. The views from the windows are of gardens and trees; there is not a studio to be seen in any direction. The rooms are low-ceilinged, compact and comfortably furnished with an eye for traditional English antiques. There are many paintings, pots, sculptures, pieces of china ornaments, and books. Small Henry Moore sculptures stand on window-sills and shelves. A linen cupboard is full of maquettes. The painting by the fireplace is by Courbet. The figure standing on a chest upstairs is a Rodin. Some small primitive figures in a cabinet would be the envy of the British Museum. The only addition to the house is a reception room with windows on three sides. It has a wall of art books and various tables smothered in a display of crystals, stones, corals, eggs, shells, and further small pieces of sculpture. There is so much to see that one only becomes gradually aware of the treasures—a beautiful Romanesque carving from an Italian church, a massive pastel drawing by Degas, another plump Courbet, a drawing by Ruskin, a very solid sketch of bathers by Cézanne, a bulbous Congo death mask, an Aztec head, a 13th-century English jug, a Mycenaean figurine, an Eskimo whalebone carving, and a lithe Persian lynx with one leg missing.

Moore himself is a rather stocky figure, with a distinctly "sporty" air. He is modest, almost shy, with a boyish sense of fun and sharp, twinkling

Moore and daughter Mary at the holiday home in Forte dei Marmi, Italy.
He has always been good at winning games, especially table tennis.

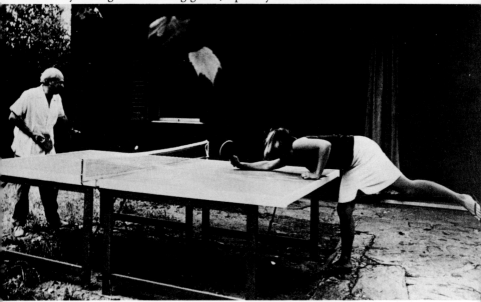

blue eyes. He dresses in good traditional English clothes—sports jackets, flannel trousers, neat blue shirts with matching ties—definitely a country man or a farmer, one might think. He has never displayed a taste for jeans, polo-neck pullovers or bow-ties. Even in the '30s, when a fashion for all things "French" was *de rigueur* in English intellectual circles, he never affected to wear a beret, as did both Ben Nicholson and my father Herbert Read. At lunchtime, he enjoys cold meat and pickles, washed down with a bottle of stout, and each guest will have his own bottle standing in a silver dish with his own bottle-opener alongside.

Such things are superficial aspects of character; much more to the point are the things that you only discover in time. Moore has always been good at winning games and few people have been able to beat him at table tennis. He can juggle expertly with three balls. His hands are always busy, rubbing his knee, reaching for objects or holding the arm of his chair. He always carries a tape measure in his pocket, just as a writer carries a pen. His sense of shape, dimension, weight and numbers is uncanny. Whatever else may be going on, the measuring part of his mind

Seated figure on stone. A young
Henry Moore relaxing on the
Yorkshire Moors.

is never at rest. I remember a dinner with him in a local hotel after a long day's filming in Italy. As the Chianti sank in the bottle, Moore claimed to be able to judge the circumference of the head of each person at the table. He passed judgement on each one of us in turn, and out came the tape measure to prove the point. With six people present, he was never more than a quarter of an inch out. Our party then moved into the sedate lounge where, to the amazement of the other guests, England's greatest sculptor was to be found measuring every piece of furniture in sight, to prove to us that his estimates were right. On another occasion, probably in response to some query I made as to the reasons for dividing the re-clining figures into separate parts, or perhaps to explain why he made models of his ideas rather than drawings, he quickly emptied a dish of potato crisps and began to arrange them in a series of undeniably Moore*ish* forms, ringing endless changes on the same pieces as sculpture followed sculpture on the coffee table.

Moore is a man of exceptional intellectual and emotional energy. Controlled energy of this kind is the power behind all great art. I have rarely seen Moore lose his temper. I remember an occasion when he was indignant about a proposal to turn an airfield near his home into one of London's major airports. He had drafted a letter to *The Times* which his secretary had seen fit to moderate for his approval. He saw reason in this, but the restrictions on his feelings revived all his intense anger. He was about to give expression to this, but thinking better of it, he seized a broom and began to sweep savagely a spotless studio floor. Feeling was translated into action, which is what a sculptor's job is all about.

No one could be more patient with an interviewer. He enjoys talking about his work but can never be drawn into public discussion of his contemporaries. Sometimes his simple and persuasive explanations arouse a slight suspicion that his perfectly correct and plausible statements conceal a complexity that can only be revealed in his work. It is as though he wanted to defend himself from self-awareness. If you ask him a question in a tentative or hesitant way, he will sense a muddle in your mind, but he is far too polite to say so. "What you mean is . . ." he replies firmly, and then goes on to make a positive assertion, which immediately dis-perses and replaces one's own tentative enquiry. The tables have been turned and one hardly notices. He is a stickler for truth and has an unshakeable belief in the rightness of his own opinion, a belief strong enough to entirely erase any sense of contradiction in his views.

I doubt if any visitor to Moore's studio has left without feeling the sense of purpose that pervades the whole place. However strange Moore's sculptures may seem to someone who expects all art to be a mirror held up to nature, there is a remarkable unity between the landscape, the workshops and what has been made in them. At the centre is the man himself, and his profound but unassertive convictions about human experience.

"We would," he once told me, "feel differently if we were horses, if we went about on four legs and slept standing up. All our sense of art, of architecture would be different—of course it would!" Elsewhere he has said:

> The things I like most in art are marked by deep human understanding. I like art to give more than an everyday feeling. I don't think that we shall or should ever get away from the thing that all sculpture is based on in the end: the human body. The child, learning to see, first distinguishes only two-dimensional shapes. It cannot judge distances or depths. Later, for its own personal safety and practical needs, it has to develop (partly by means of touch) the ability to judge roughly three-dimensional distances. But having satisfied the requirements of practical necessity, most people go no further. They do not make the further intellectual and emotional effort needed to comprehend form in all its full special existence. That is what the sculptor must do. He gets the solid shape inside his head. He thinks of it, whatever its size, as if he were holding it completely enclosed in the hollow of his hand. He knows while he looks at one side what the other side is like; he identifies himself with its centre of gravity, its mass, its weight. He realizes its volume as the space that the shape displays in the air.

Moore knows that all life evolves as a balance of forces. The shapes we find in nature are consequences of such thrusts and tensions. They are vital structures that make growth and evolution possible. The processes of change, so inevitable to the survival of life, are as essential to art. Art that does not evolve from its own ancestry cannot stay alive for long.

You might as well say, why is it necessary to have art at all?—because you can't have something that stops. It's like saying, why is it necessary for science to go on? Why can't we be satisfied with the flat earth theory? This is the growth of human intelligence, sensitivity and so on. Things must change—you just can't go on repeating. The visual arts are a few people—the practising artists, devoting their life to their art—and if they don't make a change, then they are doing nothing.

Moore's statements come directly from his deepest instincts. Nothing is said for effect or "put on". Once we were filming the process of cutting up an immense sculptural maquette that had taken nearly nine months to complete. The sculpture had to be sliced like a cheese in order to load the portions onto a lorry. Moore left this delicate piece of surgery to the experts and went to his one o'clock lunch as work continued. As a crane lifted the top section out of its position at the peak of a gigantic ring, it was obvious that the piece was slightly off-balance. It swung on the end of the crane and crashed into the adjacent second part of the sculpture. Pieces of plaster and wood fell to the floor. We all stood by, appalled by the disaster. Moore, summoned from his lunch, rode down from his house on a bicycle and assessed the situation at a glance. "It can be mended —I mean that's what life is—sometimes you purposely destroy a thing to make something else out of it. Art is not a process of just gradual perfection. You have accidents, you have troubles, you have difficulties, you destroy things, you discard something. You make a new thing—and all this—this is the way you live, you take the rough with the smooth."

A view of Castleford today. Moore spent the first 21 years of his life there, before moving to London.

CHAPTER TWO
THE EARLY DAYS

Those who live in the North of Britain scorn the Southerner. The Lancashire painter, L. S. Lowry, said of his work that it was about "the battle of life". Certainly this awareness of struggle and this determination to win is an ingrained characteristic. Farming is hard, the weather often ferocious or bleak, and the landscape is remote and awe-inspiring. Factories and mills lie in deep valleys, and homes climb up steep hillsides to wind-swept ridges. Mining is a part of this hard northern tradition and Henry Moore was born in a mining family. His father was of Irish stock and came from Lincolnshire. His mother was from Staffordshire. There were eight children in the family.

Moore's father started work at the age of nine. When he moved to Castleford in Yorkshire, he started in the pit. The first family home was at 30 Roundhill Road, a typical red-brick terraced back-to-back house, which has now been demolished. It had a cellar, two rooms up and two rooms down. There was a backyard with an earth closet, leading to a lane lined with similar backyards on the opposite side. On Mondays the lanes would be hung with washing right across the street from end to end. On other days they were ideal places for children's games, interrupted by the passage of sewage carts, the wagons delivering free coal and the tradesmen making their calls. The front side of the house would be "the respectable side", with a smart front door and a well-scrubbed doorstep. The front parlour window presented to the world the best quality lace curtains. The room was used only on Sundays and for visitors, and had a piano in it. The back room was everything else: living-room, kitchen, bathroom, and the whole family would be gathered in front of the kitchen range and around the table where the customary high tea would be served every day. In the winter evenings everyone joined in making rugs out of pieces of scrap fabric sewn together on a frame. A large family, living in such close quarters, usually develops strong qualities of loyalty, intimacy, self-reliance and powers of concentration. Anything else would be impossible.

There was a strong atmosphere of self-education and self-improvement in the family. Moore's father taught himself mathematics and literature. He learned to play the violin and passed examinations which enabled him to improve his situation in the mine. He became a "deputy" and qualified to be an under-manager, though his health prevented him from taking the job. In a photograph, he is seen as a short, stocky figure, a little stern

(*above*) It was in a small terraced house similar to these in
Castleford that Henry Moore grew up. The actual house
was pulled down some years ago.

24

of countenance and proud and determined in his stance. His interests extended to wider fields than self-improvement and one of his friends, who was a visitor to the house, was Herbert Smith, the first President of the Yorkshire Miners' Union. During a long miners' strike Moore remembers his father sitting in the light that filtered through the cellar grating, making chairs and mending shoes.

Father: Raymond Spencer Moore.   Mother: Mary Baker Moore.

Amongst the pictures in the house was a framed reproduction of Holman Hunt's religious painting, *The Light of the World*, a detail of which Moore remembered forty years later whilst drawing miners with their lamps walking back from the coal-face in the Castleford colliery during the Second World War.

Two of Moore's sisters and a brother became teachers and his father wished him to do the same. It was the only obvious way to escape from a future down the pit. Moore went to the local primary school and to Sunday school at the nearby Non-Conformist chapel. All the children were sent to church on Sunday morning. Moore remembers that it was at Sunday school that he first heard of Michelangelo. At the age of eleven he had already formed the idea of becoming a famous sculptor.

Moore failed his grammar school examinations the first time, but his father made him sit them again. At the Castleford grammar school he was exceptionally fortunate in the fact that a new art mistress, Miss Gostick, was appointed. She immediately recognized the boy's talents and offered him every help and encouragement. Her brightest pupils were invited to her home on Sunday afternoons, and there she showed them copies of

Castleford Grammar School Art
Class. Moore (holding pot) with
teacher, Miss Gostick, alongside.

The Studio magazine. It was the only publication in England at that time
which kept its readers up to date with developments in art at home and
abroad. At the school Moore was able to do pottery, carve the lettering
on the roll of honour, write a play, and design covers for the school
magazine. The headmaster had a keen interest in architecture and organized excursions to nearby churches at Adel and Methley.

Gargoyle from Methley Parish
Church, near Castleford, visited by
Moore when a student.

In Castleford itself there was less of interest to see, apart from the great slagheap that dominated the town like a mountain, but the countryside was only a few streets away. During Moore's school holidays and his latter student days in Leeds, there was time to explore the more dramatic parts of the Yorkshire landscape a little further afield. This was a world of sweeping moors and strange formations of weathered rocks.

The river-beds were full of stones and boulders, beautifully shaped and worn smooth by the force of the water. Such beauty spots were famous and much visited by people brought up in the 19th-century romantic tradition. It is hardly chance that the shape of Henry Moore's first *Two Piece Reclining Figure*, 1959 has a remarkable resemblance to a huge outcrop of rock at Adel, where Moore's headmaster had taken him to see the carvings in the church nearly half a century before.

It would be easy, in search of formative influences, to give an impression of Moore at this time as a dedicated scholar consciously looking at the world around him for signs and indications which would determine the way his sculpture would develop. This, I think, is far from the case. Moore recalls these things in retrospect, just as he now remembers childhood games with pieces of stick and carved wood, or the little clay oven that they used to make to keep their hands warm, or going to the abattoir and watching men killing a bull and making a hole in its skull in order to put in a stick to stir up its brains. Some of Moore's sculptures have strangely divided heads and there is a long series of works that take the form of a skull or helmet, with a second mysterious object inside. One of my own strongest recollections of Castleford is of a butcher's shop, its window crammed with massive lumps of bright red flesh and piles of gleaming white knuckle-bones.

During his school days visual impressions were pouring into his mind and being absorbed without any conscious awareness of their worth. The eye was alert, yet innocent. A drawing done as late as 1918 shows no sign at all of his distinctive vision. It's very much in the manner of Aubrey Beardsley and other illustrators influenced by the Art Nouveau style. As the 1914-18 war began, Henry Moore was reading Thomas Hardy, D. H. Lawrence and Dostoevsky. His father had raised no fundamental objections to his son's awkward desire to be a sculptor, but insisted that he qualified as a teacher first. So, by 1916, the 18-year-old Moore found

A drawing by Moore in 1918, clearly
influenced by Aubrey Beardsley.

himself still in Castleford as a student teacher in his own elementary school. What was determining Moore's future at this stage of his life was the wish of both himself and his art teacher, Miss Gostick, to make the most of what the Yorkshire educational system had to offer. She had already been in touch with the chief art inspector in the area to ensure that Moore followed the correct procedures and won the relevant scholarships. His progress from a student teaching job in Castleford to a place at the Leeds School of Art, and then at the Royal College of Art in London, was carefully planned.

The war placed all this at risk. Moore seems to have had none of the qualms of conscience suffered by some of the artistic young men of his generation. He was as patriotic and eager as the next man. He enlisted in the 15th London Regiment (Civil Service Rifles) and was happy enough to be training in and around London, where he could visit for the first time those happy hunting-grounds of his, the National Gallery and the British Museum. In 1917 he was posted overseas as a machine gunner, and nearly suffered the same fate that overtook Gaudier-Brzeska. Brzeska, a few years older than Moore, was perhaps the only other sculptor living in England who might in the future have equalled Moore's achievements. He was killed in action.

Henry Moore in The Great War. He was gassed during the fighting at Cambrai.

Moore was involved in an action at Cambrai, in France, which left only 42 out of 400 men alive. Moore, though gassed, was one of the survivors and was demobilized in 1919. He resumed his teaching, which he hated, and then with the help of an ex-servicemen's grant and with the backing already prepared by Miss Gostick, he gained a place at the Leeds School of Art. His education in art began in earnest. "I would have to catch an 8 a.m. train from Castleford to Leeds and get to the School of Art before 9.30. The day's timetable was then 9.30 till one o'clock, and two o'clock till four, and then a break till 7 p.m., and from 7 p.m. to 9 p.m. were evening classes. So I would leave at 9.00 and be home about 11.00. And then you would have to do 'animals in action' or 'perspective' which was homework, so that it would probably be about half-past twelve before one got to bed. I didn't mind this, and that period between 4.00 and 7.00 was a wonderful time where one could go to the reference library in Leeds and look up books. It was there that I came across Roger Fry's *Vision and Design*. This was a great opening of one's eyes to things."

Moore with his great fr
fellow artist Raymond (
Leeds, 1921.

CHAPTER THREE
OPENING EYES

Roger Fry was the English art critic most responsible for bringing English art lovers up to date with ideas that had already been current in Paris for twenty years or more. It was Fry who made his readers look again at the collections of carvings in the non-English section of the world's museums, and see them as works of art rather than interesting relics of savage cultures. Fry saw, in what had until then been regarded as "primitive" art, qualities of form and expressiveness absent in the "civilized" tradition of Greek and Roman cultures. Copying this tradition, Fry might well have argued, was not creating. What he admired in primitive and medieval arts, was a quality of vitality and power that came from carvers who could express deeply felt emotions directly in terms of the materials and the tools they used. Such works might be disconcerting but they possessed an inner life, whereas academic art was dead.

English painting too was in the doldrums, though it had gone through certain stages of evolution for which there had been no counterpart in sculpture. It had turned back to a detailed study of nature, which combined a realistic style with religious and moral purposes.

It was a strange mixture of eroticism and medieval pageantry. Then came the sinuous and decorative forms of the Art Nouveau style, blended with an intelligent appraisal of Japanese print design. Some of the concepts of Impressionism were adapted to English light and English temperament by artists such as Walter Sickert and his companions in the New English Art Club. When Sickert and his friends were joined by one of England's few cubist painters, Wyndham Lewis, to form the Camden Town Group, Lewis's aggression was somewhat diminished by Sickert's delightfully Edwardian chauvinism. No woman was allowed to join the group. "There are," declared Sickert, "lots of two sex clubs, and several one sex clubs, and this is one of them." The condition of painting and sculpture was indeed a long way behind developments in Europe.

By 1912, the Italian Futurist, Boccioni, had called for "a complete renewal of this mummified art". In Moscow, in 1920, the sculptor Naum Gabo brought out his "Realist Manifesto", calling for a new constructivist sculpture based on science, space and abstraction. In 1914 Gaudier-Brzeska published a manifesto in Wyndham Lewis's Vorticist magazine *Blast*, in which he roundly declared: "Sculptural energy is the mountain, sculptural feeling is the appreciation of masses in relation,

Constantin Brancusi with Moore in
Paris, 1945.

Herbert Read. 1936.

William Rothenstein. Self-portrait 1930.

Roger Fry. Late self-portrait.

Augustus John. Self-portrait *circa* 1901.

sculptural ability is the defining of these masses by planes." Elsewhere in that same year, he implied that only he, Epstein and Brancusi fully understood the possibilities of woods, stones and metals. Brancusi had by then reduced the human head to the form of a highly-polished egg. Epstein was working on equally pure carvings in marble, the smooth geometric forms of which suggested animals and birds. Between 1913 and 1918 he attempted to apply the methods of Cubism to a sculpture called *Rock Drill*. This stylized figure of a man with a pneumatic drill, cast in metal, represented a modernist interest in the forms of machinery and industrial equipment. In 1913 Marcel Duchamp had exhibited a bicycle wheel as a sculpture and Picasso had made figures out of discovered objects. By a process of metamorphosis he transformed them into uncanny presences with undeniably human attributes. By 1920, just as Moore was beginning his second year at Leeds, the Russian sculptor, Archipenko, had made a standing figure from a sequence of triangles, arcs and holes, totally devoid of any kind of classical method or intention. The new freedom and this will for experiment and self-expression were not widely known in England until Roger Fry organized his famous exhibition "Manet and the Post-Impressionists" in 1911. It included works by Matisse, Picasso, Van Gogh, Gauguin and Cézanne, which were seen in London for the first time.

Provincial art schools were hardly the place for challenging the established conventions of the time. Moore was depressed by what he found. A slavish teaching of rules and methods devoted to the meticulous renderings of tone and photographic appearance. Dismal plaster-cast copies of Greek and Roman originals, covered in whitewash and dust, which had to be dutifully copied by the student, meant nothing to him. "Who is wrong?" he asked himself. "Is it me or them?"

The moment of doubt passed, and he continued his studies. The emphasis was on academic drawing. The school had no sculpture teacher and a graduate fresh from the College of Art was appointed especially to teach Moore. Most of the work was modelling and copying; carving was not taught at the time. But his teachers could at least get him through the exams and help him to develop his eye and his technical ability. He won a scholarship to London with a drawing of a pair of hands, that so impressed the examiners that it was passed round the local Yorkshire schools for years afterwards, as an example of what to do to please the Board of Education.

However, it was in Leeds that Moore had his first opportunity to experience modern art at first hand. The Vice-Chancellor of Leeds University, Sir Michael Sadler, owned a first-rate collection of African carvings and of modern art, including works by Cézanne, Gauguin, Matisse and Kandinsky. He often invited students to his home to discuss with him what they saw. Moore's closest friend at Leeds was the painter Raymond Coxon, who had been with him at Castleford and who went with him to the Royal College of Art in London. They remained close friends until separated during the Second World War when Moore moved out of London.

Moore won his scholarship to the Royal College of Art in 1921. In terms of ideas, imagination and sensibility, he was in the difficult situation of being way ahead of most of his teachers and professors. Fortunately the Rector at the College, Sir William Rothenstein, the son of a Yorkshire wool merchant, was a man of wide sympathies and some insight. He had been a friend of Degas, Oscar Wilde and Aubrey Beardsley. He was, Moore says, "Not a provincial and brought in as a new broom". Moore's connection with the college continued for eleven years until the end of 1931, first as student, then as teacher. These were the formative years of his life, and also the most difficult. One of his professors remarked, pointing to one of his drawings: "This man has been feeding on garbage." After gaining his Diploma, he had a year of advanced studies and a travelling scholarship that took him to Italy.

On his return Rothenstein appointed him to the College staff as an instructor for seven years. Rothenstein told him: "You have the ball at your feet." The job gave Moore enough security to make ends meet, and to buy sufficient material to carve small sculptures in freedom during his spare time. In the vacations he could make trips to Paris, often with Raymond Coxon, to see what was going on there. He had letters of introduction to artists and collectors provided by Rothenstein. These were not always used. Arriving at the door of Maillol's studio, he said to himself: "Oh well, he's working and won't want to see me", and turned away. He did visit Pellerin's collection of Cézannes in 1923. As the door of the house opened, he saw immediately in front of him the majestic

Grandes Baigneuses, now in the Philadelphia Museum of Art. "It was," he said, "like seeing Chartres for the first time."

In 1929 he married Irina Radetzky, who was a student of painting at the College, and they moved to Hampstead, where he later had the use of one of a row of studios where Ben Nicholson and Barbara Hepworth also worked. Irina's Austrian father had been killed in the war and her Russian mother, who had remarried, lost touch with her. She was educated in the Crimea and went to Moscow to train for the ballet. Her mother traced her there and a Polish courier took her to Paris to continue her education. She came to England in 1921 and was given a home at Marlow, in Buckinghamshire, by the father of her mother's second husband.

Artists' holiday in Norfolk, 1931.
(*l. to r.*) Ivon Hitchens, Irina Moore,
Henry Moore, Barbara Hepworth,
Ben Nicholson, and friend.

At the Royal College of Art, Rothenstein had a custom of organizing Sunday dinner parties and Moore, whilst still a student, found himself mixing with celebrities such as T. S. Eliot and E. M. Forster. Once he found himself standing by the fire with Ramsay MacDonald and thought: "If this is the Prime Minister of England, then I can be anything!"

He had exhibited in a mixed show in 1926 and this brought him in contact with Epstein. In 1928 Moore's first one-man show sold £90 worth of sculptures and 30 drawings at £1 each. Both Augustus John, the painter, and Epstein bought one, and this support from two of the most famous artists in England was a valuable boost to Moore's morale. The exhibition was favourably reviewed by Herbert Read in *The Listener*, but elsewhere a considerable body of criticism was building up against him. It was part of a far more general battle that was being fought at the time between the supporters of modern art and the supporters of the Royal Academy, both in private and in the Press. As one reviewer put it: "Mr Moore, an accomplished workman, should be able to produce frankly realistic sculpture. It would enable him to find his own level again, and eventually substitute his own researches for an ill-digested medley of other people's."

Nevertheless, in the same year, Moore got his first public commission for a large relief figure representing *North Wind*, which was to be placed safely beyond the reach of most critics on the top of the new London Transport headquarters in Victoria.

Moore's next exhibition was at the premises of one of London's leading dealers of modern art, the Leicester Galleries in Leicester Square. The catalogue preface was written by Epstein who declared: "This sculptor is a liberator of the spirit. Before these works I ponder in silence. Their vast disproportions throw the shadow of our fears upon the background of space . . . secret forces ready to burst forth on earth to startle the unthinking out of their complacency. For the future of sculpture in England, Henry Moore is vitally important." The exhibition earned Moore £385. In the same year the first article on his work was published abroad and he also made his first sale to a foreign gallery, when a Hamburg museum bought a small carved head for £8.

These encouraging factors were matched by equal difficulties. The London *Morning Post* was an influential newspaper and their art critic

Seated girl and heads from 1926 sketchbook. Pen and ink, chalk, wash. Page inscribed 'breasts good'.

a girls love
Beast's End.

had little sympathy for Epstein's opinion. He wrote: "The cult of ugliness thrives at the hand of Mr Moore. He shows utter contempt for the natural beauty of women and children, and in doing so deprives every stone of its value as a means of aesthetic and emotional expression. Aesthetic detachment is bound to atrophy soul and vision and lead to revolting formlessness such as offends sensitive people." The review revived the controversy about Moore at the Royal College. The professor who was then head of the department in which Moore taught took the article to Rothenstein, asking for Moore's dismissal, and the old students' association passed a resolution adding their weight to this demand. Moore and Rothenstein held their ground but by 1931 Moore's contract was near to its end. The following year he accepted a new post as Head of the Department of Sculpture at the Chelsea School of Art.

An account of the events during those eleven years hardly represents what was really going on in the mind of Henry Moore between 1921 and 1931. For the last hundred years no one could easily answer the questions: "How do I paint a picture? How do I make a sculpture? What is a work of art meant to be?" In Ancient Greece, in classical Rome, during the Middle Ages, and in Renaissance Florence, for example, the answers could be given. The apprenticed artist, working in his Master's studio, was told what to do and how to do it. But our modern culture has split into more and more divisions and specializations. Anyone interested in art, either as a spectator or a practitioner, is exposed to a continually expanding quantity of visual experience, as films, books, photographs, museums, galleries and the researches of scholars explore and expound every nook and cranny of observable information. Our visual awareness has also been enriched by a vast source of new images derived from flight, speed, mechanical and technical machinery, and electronics. Microphotography can show us the smallest particles of nature and most minute manifestations of life. In addition to all this, we have changed our attitudes to many aspects of human experience. There are fewer moral taboos. Psychologists of various schools have made us aware of previously unknown areas in the workings of our minds and emotions. Educationalists have altered our evaluation of childhood self-expression. There have been attempts to make a science of aesthetics, and lacking a widely held religious framework to our lives, we have turned to art as a provider for our spiritual needs.

Moore has always been well aware that he was born at a time when everything was being thought out anew. The years between 1921 and 1931 were not too long a time for an artist to spend searching for his bearings, assimilating what he needed, and rejecting what was not true to his nature. An artist such as Moore acts, I would suggest, by a process of empathy. He was bound to reject some kinds of sculptural activity. For example, the Albert Memorial is a certain type of cultural rationalization. The only truly imaginative part of it is the vast Gothic fantasy that Gilbert Scott created to shelter the 15-foot (4·7 m) high. Prince Albert seated underneath. Other sculptors were engaged to carve the 178 figures of artists and men of letters applied to the base of the monument to symbolize an artistic tradition originating in the age of Pericles and culminating in the Victorian period. At the four corners stand groups representing Agriculture, Manufacture, Commerce and Engineering, and well beyond their reach further piles of animals and figures symbolize the four continents of Europe, Asia, Africa and America. Yet the lack of force and power in this assembly of bureaucratic pictorial art makes it now a rather sad example of concepts that have lost their validity. The art that was used to express these concepts, not having an imaginative power of its own, cannot still be exciting. Yet the whole purpose of art schools—such as those at Leeds and the Royal College—had been to train artists in that kind of work.

It was also the custom to enhance parks and open spaces with statues and fountains, which added nobility and decorum to the pleasures of contemplating flowerbeds and trees. Ingenious constructions involved cherubs, dolphins and water-nymphs, whose forms supported stout basins richly decorated with wreaths and floral motifs. Further columns of figures and carvings rose to a point from which the cascade emanated out of a fish's mouth. The best of them called for considerable skill and craftsmanship. The designs were vaguely derived from the elaborate work of 15th-century goldsmiths and silversmiths in Nuremberg. Such motifs and forms could be assembled from pattern books, just as effectively as any kind of 18th-century decoration could be painted or plastered onto a ceiling designed in the manner of Robert Adam.

Moore's father would no doubt assume that a sculptor would be a maker of such fantasies, or of generals on horseback, statesmen on plinths, or Lord Mayors proudly situated beside banks and town halls. Should none of these concepts appeal, then at least a sculptor could be expected to do a decent portrait or make an alabaster lady, discreetly nude or graciously attired, to add a touch of luxury to a rich man's home.

Sculpture is still very much associated with such purposes in the public mind, and its style has always been far more restricted than that of painting. Within the immediate span of his youthful experience Moore could probably only name Rodin, Degas and Epstein as men who thought of sculpture as an art rather than a profession. During that period Moore was extending his knowledge of sculpture in every possible way by studying what could be seen in the British Museum, in contemporary Paris, and in the cities of Italian Renaissance. He writes in a sketchbook: "Remember the world tradition", which suggests that he was looking at every piece of evidence he could find, of sculpture whose shape he found moving, expressive and alive.

The head of the Virgin, which he carved from marble in 1923, is only 21 inches (53 cm) high. Possibly it was one of the things that helped him to get his diploma at the College and it was bought by his friend Raymond Coxon. It is a copy of a 14th-century Florentine sculpture in the Victoria and Albert Museum. Dignified, serene, tender—the original is a sensitive work, and Moore's copy shows that he could have excelled in an academic career and might well have become a youthful President of the Royal Academy.

Moore of course was doing what most students have done since: working at school in the ways that would satisfy their teachers, whilst at the same time privately doing their own thing at home. The 1923 Virgin does nothing to prepare one for the *Mother and Child* sculpture that he began only a year later. Moore has explained that in the early days the problem was how to fit his ideas within the odd pieces of stone that he could afford to buy, which were often much smaller than he would have wished and awkwardly shaped. Without a proper studio he was severely limited in the scale of work that could be managed, and so many of his carvings in the '20s are heads of various kinds, only a few inches high, not much larger than a fair-sized pebble, and often as smooth and rounded as such pebbles might be. The *Mother and Child* is 22½

The Head of the Virgin, 1922
One of the earliest surviving sculptures
by Henry Moore, after a 14th-century
relief by Domenico Rosselli.

Madonna and Child, 1925
Work on this was interrupted by
Moore's visit to Italy in 1925.

inches (57 cm) high, yet it appears massive and monumental. The looming bulging nature of the stone itself is emphasized rather than diminished by the sculptor cutting into it. The bent elbow of the lower arm has an immense stumpy strength to it. The mother's face is buried within the forms. The representation of character in the faces is as minimal as in a Picasso painting or an African mask. Moore was obviously strongly influenced by so-called primitive African or Mexican examples when he began it, but before it was finished, he had been to Italy.

He had gone reluctantly and though his travels through the great art museums of the Renaissance were diligent, he wished at times to be back in England. He wrote in a letter that he longed for the sight of a good thick English tree. All the same, the works of Massaccio, Giotto, Michelangelo and Donatello made a deep impression on him, even if he did not want to admit it at the time. Every day in Florence he spent ten minutes in front of Massaccio's *Tribute Money* before looking at anything else. The "dead" art of the Renaissance, only seen in reproduction and judged from poor casts and copies, was, in reality, startlingly alive. These new influences, about which he has often spoken many years later, had, in 1925, to be firmly thrust into the background before he could finish the abandoned *Mother and Child* on his return.

In the '20s Moore was almost entirely a carver of wood and stone, thereby rejecting the emphasis on modelling taught in the schools. His figures included various seated and standing works, as well as torsos and further sculptures on the theme of mother and child. A beautiful little alabaster carving of a baby at its mother's breast is only $7\frac{1}{2}$ inches (19 cm) high. It is probably as abstract as any of his surviving work before 1930. It is a smoother and far more sensuous variation of a voracious and aggressive child carved in a rough textured stone in 1927. The child at the breast is typical of Moore's constant intimate sense of humanity, fertility and motherhood.

This sculpture's highly attractive surface no doubt pays tribute to Brancusi. But there is nothing cold or chromium-plated about Moore's shapes, which remain clearly of flesh and blood. In this little sculpture he had already learned to establish a satisfying relationship between two separate forms contained in a single carving. All these early works are evidence of a great talent searching for a central core of belief.

The greatest single theme of Moore's sculptural life, and the one for which he is best known, is the reclining figure. The end of this first period of his work produced an astonishing concentration of figures, beginning with a mature and womanly sculpture which Moore cast himself in concrete in 1927. By now Moore was developing strong attitudes to his use of materials, to the difference between carving and modelling sculpture, and to the dangers of the materials themselves being too sweet and seductive for the shapes of the sculptures to be appreciated in their own right. A certain stern independence had begun to assert itself. He defined his attitude to sculpture when he wrote in 1934, three years after ending his association with the Royal College of Art:

> For me a work must first have a vitality of its own. I do
> not mean a reflection of the vitality of life, of movement, of
> physical action, frisking dancing figures and so on, but that
> a work can have in it the pent-up energy, an intense life of
> its own, independent of the object it may represent. When
> work has this powerful vitality, we do not connect the word
> beauty with it. Beauty in the later Greek or Renaissance
> sense, is not the aim of my sculpture. Because a work of art
> does not aim at reproducing natural appearances it is not
> therefore an escape from life but may be a penetration into
> reality, not a sedative or a drug, not just the exercise of good
> taste, the provision of pleasant shapes and colours in a pleas-
> ing combination, not a decoration to life, but an expansion
> of the significance of life, a stimulation to a greater effort in
> living.

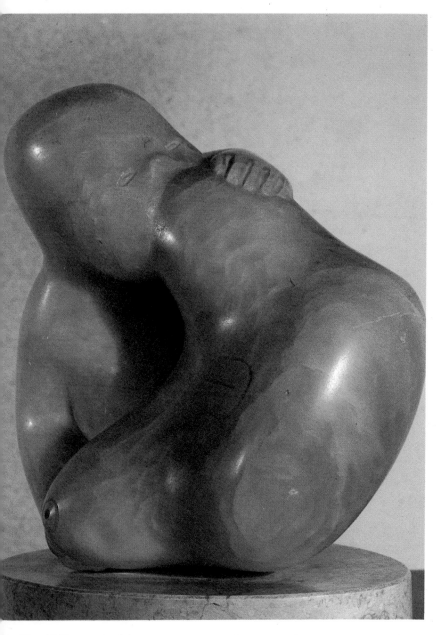

Suckling Child, 1930, in alabaster.

CHAPTER FOUR
DRAWING CONCLUSIONS

Moore sometimes writes as though there were a battle to be won, as though survival depended on a yet greater will to win. What is the nature of this struggle? He told me once that he was a sculptor because he wanted to make things real. As realism in the generally accepted sense is not the first thing that comes to mind when looking at some of his sculptures, this is yet another of Moore's seemingly simple explanations that needs further consideration. A sculptor is like a builder, and to speak of "making real" is to say that what exists in the mind has no reality until it becomes a three-dimensional object. To Moore, such objects, made real, are not replicas of things seen. They are embodiments of things felt and things conceived. From time to time he has drawn animals. He thinks of them in terms of physical qualities rather than as visual phenomena. He talks of the power of shapes, rather than about the qualities of outline, light or colour.

Animals can teach you all sorts of things about sculptural form, which you would not get so clearly from anything else. I've often studied the gorilla at the zoo, and for me the gorilla has more sense of power, of physical strength than the lion or a tiger or other animals that people ordinarily think are more gracious and stronger. The backview of a gorilla is to me the essence of physical strength, of tremendous pent-up reserve of power. An elephant is very different. An elephant has this power, but there is a kind of gentle slowness. You feel that an elephant could stand forever like a rock. A rhinoceros has a very aggressive look to it. It's like a tank that's going to attack.

Moore is using adjectives that might just as well describe his sculptures and drawings. It also illustrates how he looks at human beings. The drawing of an old man which he did at college in 1921 is one of his rare conventional studies, and one of the very few portraits that he has ever made. It shows Moore's ability to excel at what he was taught to do. The face is described by tone and the conventional shading in pencil is done with parallel hatching and cross hatching. The portrait of his mother, made in 1927, is another rare example of a work where he has concentrated on the actual appearance and personality of the sitter, using pencil, pen and black wash; but he has manipulated the dense blacks by scraping and

rubbing with his finger to create an abstract quality of darkness and light to add power to the image.

The figure drawing of 1922 is far more characteristic. It is a study in which form predominates. The distracting details, which would describe character or personality, are almost entirely eliminated. The whiteness of the paper is modified by a bold use of pencil, chalk and watercolour, to suggest the volumes and weights which he felt in his subject. It is always worthwhile when looking at a Moore drawing to work out how he set

about his task. The seated woman, also drawn during his early days at the Royal College, is a clear example. The model was first drawn delicately in pencil. Bold areas of wash established the light and shade which suggest the volumes. Then a pen is used to firm up the impression with incisive strokes and emphasis is given to the bangles on the arm, which clearly show the cross section of the limb as it might appear in a diagram.

Moore studied and taught drawing from life for twenty years. Even now he continually emphasises the absolute necessity of this training, despite the fact he now invents his figures freely from imagination. "How on earth," he asks, "can you draw accurately what's in your head if you haven't learned to draw what is in front of your eyes?" At the Royal College Moore not only drew from the models in the sculpture classes, but also took advantage of the life classes in the painting school. The models changed their poses far more often there.

Not many other sculpture students could be bothered with the life classes and the reason was, Moore believes, that drawing showed them up. Weakness could not be easily concealed. For the same reason he considered carving to be a far greater test of a sculptor's skill than the alternative method of modelling. Anyone could apply clay to an armature and, by addition or subtraction, eventually achieve a recognizable result. When carving, if you made a mistake, there was no way of putting back what had been cut away. Another firm belief of Moore's was that unless one understood the human figure one would be unable to understand anything else, so the first step for any sculptor was to learn for himself how to master it. Nothing could be more fundamental for the artist, for the human body is oneself. It is the source of all our physical sense and emotional response to shape. It can be arranged in an infinite number of ways and as a subject for art it is the one of which we are the most acutely aware. It is the pull of gravity on our body that ties us to the earth. We have an instinctive awareness of the feel of flesh and blood, the tension of the muscles and the vulnerability of soft and sensitive areas such as the brain. The human body is the only subject on which everyone is an authority.

It is not just a matter of academic training. You can't understand it without being emotionally involved. It really is a ·deep, strong, fundamental struggle to understand one-

Seated Woman, 1921
Pencil, pen and ink, and wash.

self as much as to understand what one is drawing. Art is the expression of an individual, personal vision. If the artist's vision is a commonplace one, he will not produce great drawings, even if he has spent all his life learning drawing. Second-rate draughtsmen repeat stereotype vision. Facility alone does not produce good drawing. In the human figure one can express more completely one's feelings about the world than in any other way.

The beauty of Moore's early life studies gains much from the simplicity and naturalness of the poses, and the forceful and direct way in which he builds up the volumes on the flat paper. A standing figure done in 1923 eliminates both the head and the feet, concentrating attention on the trunk by means of bold and vigorous strokes which often cut across each other with varying degrees of density. A few patches of paint establish the form, and the whole drawing was made by starting from the centre and working towards the edge. In places, outlines and contours are barely suggested at all. "Outlines," Moore says, "should be the outcome of the inside form, the edge of form, not the silhouette." The 1926 figure, an obsessively bulky backview, reminds me of Moore's observations about gorillas. The apparently random tangle of marks and lines has an immensely powerful effect, because one's imagination is involved at every point in interpreting the reality behind the abstraction.

Moore is always careful to keep his inventiveness and resourcefulness under control, but occasionally he cannot resist a challenge. For example, there are a number of drawings that he did in Paris in 1927. He went with a friend to a life class where the model appeared in a succession of poses which were held for ever-decreasing periods of time. The final poses lasted for only one or two minutes. The students' drawings had to be completed instantly, without pause for thought. *Standing Nude*, 1927 is one of these, made with a minimal schematic use of line and wash. "It was like a tennis player practising his backhand," Moore says.

The broad backs of Moore's models feature as much in his sculptures as in his drawings. Moore has often described how one of his earliest experiences of human form derived from the practice of rubbing his mother's back to relieve her rheumatism. The maternal nature of much of Moore's work hardly needs stating, and this childhood experience of relationship between hand, body, and emotion is perhaps the earliest element in the development of his sculptural instinct.

Standing Figure, 1923
Pencil, pen and ink, wash.

52

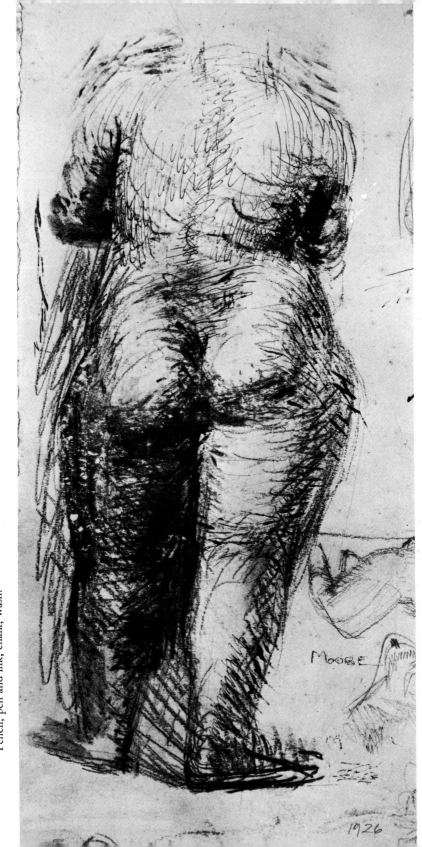

Standing Nude, 1926
Pencil, pen and ink, chalk, wash.

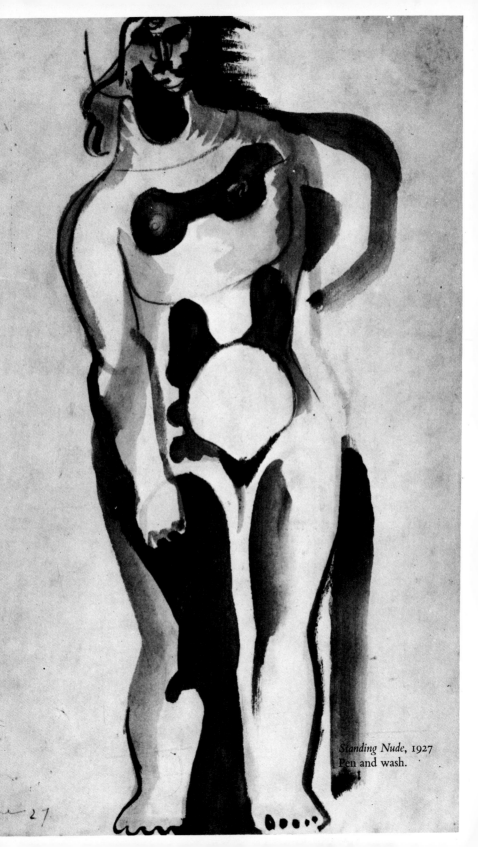

Standing Nude, 1927
Pen and wash.

Moore's drawings have a double interest. Though works of art, they were not at this stage of his life intended as such. Drawing was a method of learning. Soon it became a way of exploring sculptural ideas. To follow a line drawn by Moore with one's eye is to follow his mind. This is particularly so in a unique method of "sectional line" drawing which he began to develop as early as 1928, and which re-occurs at intervals until the present. In its simplest form it can be seen in his *Standing Nude*, 1928. His pen or pencil instead of following an outline or the level of a contour, moves at will along a horizontal or vertical section of the figure. It abruptly changes its direction to climb over a shape, leaving an up and down trail that might have been made by a fly walking over the subject. Sometimes such drawings look as though the figures were made of irregular interlocking bricks.

Moore's sketchbooks provide a continual commentary on his mental activity over the years. Some things in them are no more than notes about what he has seen or wants to remember. They are a storehouse of images to be used or not, as chance may be. Others show us the sculptor's use of thinking. Sometimes he begins to draw with no particular subject in mind, until his unconscious doodling reveals to him a visual idea which consciously seems worth developing. Figures sitting or reclining, groups such as mother and child, or an endless variety of abstract forms and constructions, appear to float onto the pages. It seems as though we are looking at objects in a vaguely indicated landscape or atmosphere. We are standing on the surface of an imaginery world which is to me far more plausible than the mechanistic robot-filled worlds popular in science fiction films. Entirely new forms of life appear to be evolving, possibly human, possibly vegetable, and sometimes mineral. At other times we seem to have dived under the sea and to be confronted by a submarine world filled with mysterious and sometimes menacing shapes.

Other sheets of paper are covered with endless variations on a theme. For example, the idea of the seated figure whose arms and legs are shown in alternative positions, or resting in various attitudes on supports of different kinds. This juxtaposition of figures and forms on a single sheet of paper, though apparently accidental, creates its own surrealist effect. As the years go by, such visual poetry is enhanced by the use of freely applied colour, which places his inventions in an imagined space or

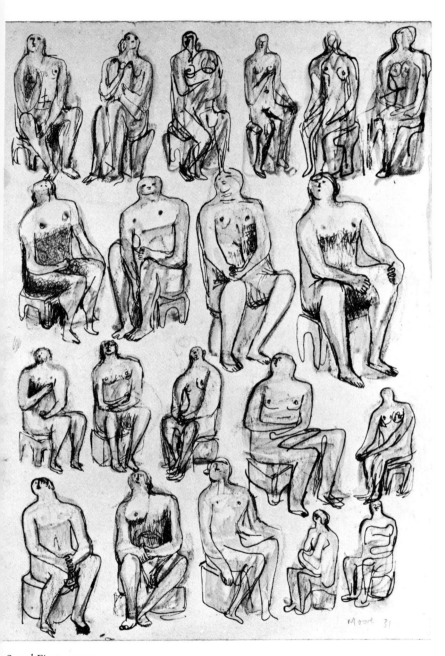

Seated Figures, 1931
Pen and ink, chalk, wash.

landscape. It is essential for a sculptor to think of his work in the round. The first view implies an equally interesting aspect from the side or from behind. The accidental effects of his techniques and the juxtapositioning of his images provide a powerful stimulus which he is quick to exploit.

Freedom is crucial to Moore's method of working on paper and he needs to work rapidly. Somewhere about 1939 he discovered the dramatic effects that could be quickly obtained by brushing a fluid watercolour over a wax crayon drawing. The wax, being water-repellent, rejected the colour in varying degrees, according to its thickness on the paper and to the density of the wash. The result gives some of his later graphic work a particularly evocative and beautiful quality. It is full of texture, grain, and mottled highlights.

Moore likes to attack his working surface with almost anything that lies to hand that can be effective: inks, "magic markers", pen, pencil, chalk, watercolour, absorbent surfaces, smudges and scrapings. He is an artist most at home when manipulating materials, just as he would do as a sculptor, building up, developing images that can be continually intensified until they have the precise effect he has in mind.

The outbreak of the Second World War was a disaster for Moore as a sculptor. Materials could not be bought. Transport could not be hired. His studio was bombed. No one wanted to buy works of art. He applied

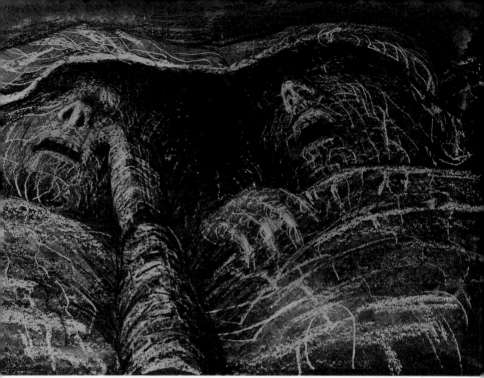

Two Sleepers, 1941 One of Moore's shelter drawings—chalk, wax
crayon, watercolour. It is reminiscent of the
sleeping apostles in Mantegna's oil-painting *The
Agony in the Garden* in the National Gallery , London.

for work in an ordnance factory as a designer of machine tools. Fortunately the application was ignored and he was invited to become a War
Artist. For the first time in his life drawing became the only outlet for his
creativity. London was suffering from some of its heaviest air-raids and
one night Moore found himself trapped in the underground railway
station near his home. Every night, 100,000 people were using these
stations as shelters. What Moore saw that night convinced him that there
was something that he could do as an artist. He accepted the offer that
had been made to him, and his shelter drawings became the most widely
popular of all his work. He made hundreds of sketches and finished
drawings, resulting in one of the most remarkable accounts of the consequences of war in the history of art. In the shelters he would simply
observe and make the most elementary drawings, as he felt shy of in-
truding on people's privacy. The next day he would fill the pages of his
sketchbook with ideas drawn from his notes and memories. Later he
would select certain sketches and base larger, fully finished drawings on
them. He did not go into the shelters as a reporter or photographer might

People sheltering in the London
Underground during the Blitz.

do; as an artist he was experiencing a vision rather than recording events. Some drawings are as richly and uniquely developed in terms of originality of technique as anything by William Blake or Samuel Palmer. Sometimes the great receding hollows of the tunnels bring to mind the swelling vortexes in some of Turner's epic paintings, or in the same artist's mysterious interiors of rooms at Petworth House. The feeling that Moore had was of both individuals and a mass of people caught in subterranean surroundings, and at the mercy of forces about which they could do nothing.

One imagined that there have never been scenes like that, so general, except perhaps when the slaves were being exported from Africa to America in the holds of slave-ships. I was trying to show my reaction to this dramatic suspense. It was like early Greek drama. It is a situation where you get the tension between people facing an impending disaster, impending doom. There is more drama in silence than in shouting. It is not action that gives drama, it's tension, it's getting the sense of things that could happen. It reminded me of the feeling I had when I was a student in Italy and discovered Massaccio.

The subject gave Moore every chance to make use of expressive forms, such as the pointed shapes of fear, the different attitudes of the relaxed sleeper and the disturbed dreamer. He only drew women and children. It was the first time that Moore had drawn the clothed figure, and the sculptural expressiveness of the female figure so dressed became a new development of his post-war sculpture. The three standing figures in Battersea Park were to be the first expression of this new outlook.

Later in the war Moore returned to his home town, Castleford, and for the first time in his life experienced the reality of going down the pit. The claustrophobic darkness horrified him and he felt deeply for the conditions that coal-face workers have to endure. He drew their tear-stained faces and white-rimmed eyes staring out of the dark, and showed the hunched-up, sweating figures on their sides hacking at the coal. He had not drawn the male figure before, nor figures in action. His full artistic response to the mining experience was longer delayed than in the case of his shelter drawings. His warrior sculptures in the mid-'50s may have

Henry Moore (r.) down the mine at
Castleford, 1942.

derived something from his experience in the mines and some of his
recent graphic work, also based on his appreciation of drawings by
Seurat and Rembrandt, show a preoccupation with forms emerging from
darkness as though illuminated by a distant lamp.

Miners' Faces, 1942. Page from *Coalmine Sketchbook.* Pen and ink, wax, crayon, wash.

with Architecture, 1943. Pen and ink, black and coloured chalks, wax crayon, wash.

ly example of architecture being incorporated into Moore's drawing.

After the war Moore no longer used drawing as a way of discovering sculpture. He started to work out his ideas directly in small-scale models that could be handled and looked at from all directions. He said that he wanted to make sculptures that were impossible to draw. He also began to increase the scale of his work. Gradually his graphic work developed independently. He made some drawings of figures in vaguely architectural settings. These might have been influenced by a visit to Greece or by recollections of Stonehenge, or by sculptural notions with which he was then engaged that involved the placing of a figure in a relationship to a wall or building. Other drawings show women who seemed to have strayed from his shelter drawings. They stand enigmatically in bare unfurnished rooms. These drawings have strong dramatic implications; they look like stage sets with actors waiting for some unwritten opera or tragedy to begin. He could be a magnificent scenic designer but he has always resisted the temptation. Once a sculpture of his appeared on stage in London as part of a memorial tribute to T. S. Eliot, but he has only once designed a set, for the production of *Don Giovanni* at the Spoleto Festival in Italy.

In the '60s Moore became very actively involved in making prints. Typically he ignored conventions and mixed techniques to gain his effects with the freedom he needed. A series of etchings drawn directly on to the plate show an elephant skull, which also inspired several sculptures. Another series of prints made marvellous use of texture and blackness to convey the effect of moonlight on Stonehenge. Some rich and densely printed lithographs illustrated the mood rather than the detail of poems by W. H. Auden. He began to rummage through his sketchbook, often going back many years. He found some slight drawings of tightrope walkers that he had jotted down at a circus in France in 1926, and made some new drawings and etchings from them. A newly perfected process of "continuous tone" lithography, which involves the use of ultra-violet light shining onto the plate through transparent sheets of drawing material, meant that he could reproduce the subtlest effects of watercolour, ink and line. He could work as he pleased directly on the transparencies and control the image at every stage in the printing. He could superimpose one image upon another and print them in any order he wished onto the same sheet of paper. Though most of his graphic work shows a preference for shades of grey, black and brown, these combinations of muted colours and lines are often printed from as many as eleven plates. One can still sense a sculptor at work, building up an image from its beginnings and intensifying its impact step by step.

The most remarkable development has been a superb series of drawings which are often made by unconventional means. Some are simple line drawings of figures, or pictures developed from a few calligraphic strokes, which suggest a subject to him. Thus abstraction becomes the source of a romantic pictorial reality. Other things are directly observed from his

Shipwreck, 1973
Pencil, charcoal, ballpoint pen, wash.

From *Sheep Sketchbook*, 1972
Ballpoint pen.

es Drawing IV, 1975 Charcoal and wash on blotting paper. A study of gnarled
ms in a hedge a few yards from Moore's studio.

own environment. There are superb drawings of his hands and of sheep, which seem to have been woven out of a single continuous looping and tangled line. He has drawn piles of logs lying outside his studio, and wintry trees and hedges that border his fields. The arthritic wood has developed obstinate and tenacious forms in which Moore finds suggestions of falling bodies and twisted crucified figures. In complete contrast to these, he has rediscovered a joy in drawing images of mother and child. His grandson is the most recent subject for an artist whose vision is never at rest.

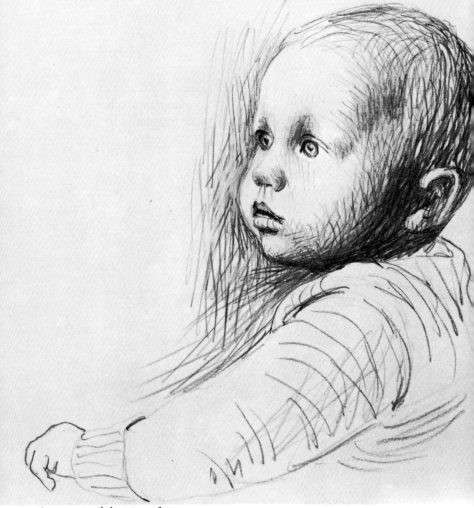

Recent pencil drawing of Henry Moore's grandson, Gus.

68

CHAPTER FIVE
BEING HIS OWN MAN

By 1931 Moore was firmly established in Hampstead. Between then and the outbreak of war this part of London became a remarkable centre of activity. Amongst the visitors to Moore's studio in those years were such leaders of the European *avant-garde* as Salvador Dali, René Magritte, Hans Arp, Moholy-Nagy and André Breton. Ben Nicholson and Barbara Hepworth lived nearby, as did Piet Mondrian for a short time. Hampstead also became a temporary home for the psychologists Sigmund Freud and Gerhardt Adler. Herbert Read was writing *Art Now* and publishing works of Carl Jung in English. An attempt was made to unite modern art with modern architecture by the founding of "Unit One". The members were Paul Nash, Hepworth, Nicholson, Edward Burra, Edward Wadsworth, Cecil Stephenson and the architects Wells Coates and Colin Lucas. Another architect, Maxwell Fry, built his glass and concrete "sun-house", and Lubetkin designed the swivelling ramps of the new penguin pool at the London Zoo. The presence of Walter Gropius stimulated the already existing interest in the German Bauhaus movement, which sought to apply modern aesthetic standards to industrial design. The chromium-plated tubular chair was invented and bent plywood furniture became fashionable. Marcel Breuer's reclining chair would have made a fitting support for one of Moore's more skeletal figures. People voiced fashionable slogans such as "Form Follows Function" and "Truth to Material". Roland Penrose, fresh from the excitements of Paris, attempted to stir up an interest in surrealist art and organized a massive exhibition in which Moore, Nash, Burra and Nicholson were placed in the company of Brancusi, Giacometti, Arp, Picasso, Ernst, Chirico, Marcel Duchamp, Picabia, Salvador Dali and André Masson.

Hampstead's intellectuals subscribed to "The Left Book Club" and took their Marxist politics and economics bound in bright orange linen covers. They read the poetry of Stephen Spender or Louis MacNeice, published in the magazine *New Verse*. In moments of relaxation, many might sneak off to the new Odeon Cinema on Haverstock Hill to see Fred Astaire and Ginger Rogers, but to do so was to be accused of patronizing kitsch. It was safer to be seen at the Hampstead Everyman watching abstract animated films by Len Lye and documentaries by John Grierson, which supported feature films by Marcel Carné, Fritz Lang or Eisenstein. The

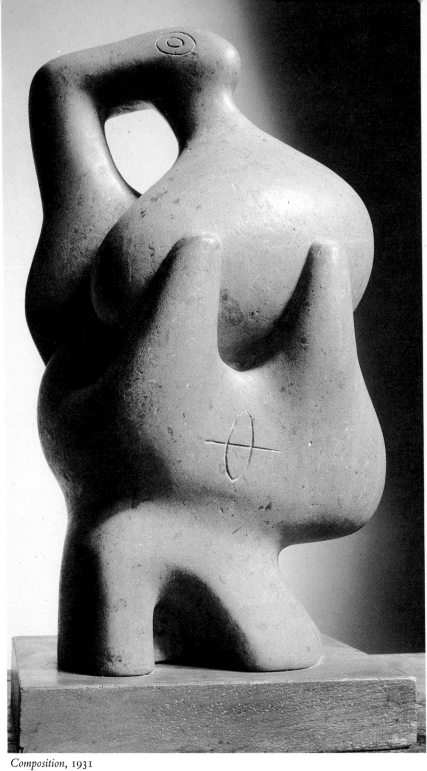

Composition, 1931

Everyman cinema first exhibited in England the works of Paul Klee in its tiny foyer gallery.

It was the heyday of "modern art". It is curious how old-fashioned that term now sounds. It was superseded by "contemporary art". Now we speak tamely of "figurative" and "non-figurative" art. The heat seems to have gone out of the battle. To be abstract is to be "academic". In the 1930s the dispute between the traditionalists and the modernists was fought with considerable bitterness. Paul Nash was on the side of the angels. His equally talented brother, John Nash, was not, having committed the unheard of sin of exhibiting at the Royal Academy. Few dealers were willing to show modern art and the purchasing policy of the Tate Gallery in the early '30s was considered by many to be lamentably cautious. The Tate bought nothing by Henry Moore until 1939, when the artist was already 41 years old.

A further cultural complication was the need that some felt to establish a bridge between art and science. This was marked by the publication of the book *Circle* in 1937, in which the views of abstract or constructivist artists such as Naum Gabo and Ben Nicholson were printed alongside statements by some of the architects already mentioned and the physicist J. D. Bernal. This heady mixture of idealism, politics, science, technology and psychoanalysis seemed to suggest that a new artistic vision could be found that was relevant to the discoveries of a brave new world. Even amongst the general public to be modern was to be fashionable. The West End showman, C. B. Cochran, was sufficiently in touch with the prevalent mood to name one of his lavish revues "Streamline".

Streamline is not a bad word to think of, when looking at some of Moore's more abstract work. The smooth flowing surfaces, continuous and unbroken, would stand up well to tests in a wind tunnel. This abstract work is only one aspect of what he was doing in the '30s, but it shows a side of his artistic nature which is still evident today. These abstract sculptures balance a more recognizably human side to his work. They show an artist who resolutely refuses to be moved off balance by the intellectual and emotional ferments around him. Moore is always his own man.

One of the sculptures that aroused much fury in his 1931 exhibition was simply titled *Composition*, 1931. It was a radical departure from the methods of some of his earlier work, and there are many influences in the piece to reward the art historian. Certain Cycladic sculptures of the period 2,000 B.C. could be quoted as representing a similar concern with purely abstract forms, showing how an artist can delight in being able to cut into and through hard stone without destroying its brittle substance, or denying its solidity and weight. The shapes in this carving please the hand as much as the eye. The whole piece is not unlike a medieval English jug.

Comparisons can also be made with some of Picasso's works. Picasso's involvement with Surrealism could be described as being the ability to bring about a metamorphosis. An object which in itself contains no particular artistic interest can, in a changed context, stand in for something else which has: a toy car can become a gorilla's head. The surrealist idea also believes in the invention by the artist of forms and shapes for which there is no exact counterpart in nature, but which have powerful associations in the unconscious mind. These ideas lead to a more general interest in shapes as they can be revealed by nature. A multitude of structures existing in bones and stones, and the natural engineering of all living growing things, can be given artistic meaning. Similar forms can be found in primitive art. Artists were becoming aware of many visual phenomena through the disclosures of the microscope and the camera. The essential belief was that whatever the artist constructed in one dimension or two should have a suggestive power that gave it vitality and expressiveness. In general, such artistic forms have been labelled by art critics as "Biomorphic". I think it is more helpful when looking at Moore's *Composition* to see in it something of the child enthusiastically clutching its mother's breast, or to think of the satisfying swelling of a gourd, or simply to recognize how three extremely beautiful shapes have been perfectly organized within a single piece of stone. Moore was perhaps comparing *Composition*, 1931 with *Mother and Child*, 1925, when he said:

> I was dissatisfied with the usual idea of direct carving in which the forms are all so embedded in each other that they don't have free and independent existence. I was trying to make this form, which is like the shape of an egg, which is the body almost completely realized though not separate from the rest. I was also getting the freedom to mix forms

and yet make an organic unit. The whole has some sort of sense of a jug. My niece, when she was very young, when she first saw this, said: 'Oh, an elephant in an armchair!' I was very pleased that she felt that it was a real object—a real person.

Shapes, to a sculptor, are what light and colour are to a painter. Many of Moore's carvings in a more or less abstract or surrealist idiom are concerned with the effects of holes and lumps that are in various ways related to human anatomy. The dark wooden carving *Composition*, 1932 has the characteristically broad crossbow-shaped expanse of shoulder from which rises a diminished and smoothed down head, which emphasizes the bulk. There is an immense feeling of physical strength in the massive forearm, which in itself almost becomes a metaphor for a child cradled at its mother's breast. The wood still bears the marks of the chisel on its slightly rippled surface. The grain is clearly exploited to show nature's way of building up a pattern of sectional lines, such as sometimes occur in his drawings. The stone *Composition* of the same year has a far less rugged appearance, and its powerful rhythms and protuberances are contained within a gleaming, polished surface from which two eyes stick out, almost like nipples. The streamline is perfect from every point of view. Like so many of Moore's sculptures, this cool piece is irresistible to the hand.

The Mother and Child, 1932 makes an interesting comparison with the 1931 jug-like composition. A degree of abstraction is very convincingly applied to this looming protective mass. It has the monumental and aloof quality that appears in much of Moore's later work.

The 1933 *Figure* is a return to the mysterious attraction of swellings and holes. Few of Moore's works give a greater satisfaction through the perfection of their surface. It is a shrouded figure, like a nurse or a nun, and has the flowing silhouette of an Arab woman wearing a djellabah. The face is no more than a tunnel burrowed into the head, but is entirely successful in suggesting a watchful personality within.

Two Forms, 1934 is one of the earliest works in which Moore separates his subject into two related parts. Symbolically the sculpture might be a Mother and Child, or a wave about to envelop a rock.

The *Four Piece Composition* of the same year has a quality of inevitability.

Three Points, 1939-40

Bird Basket, 1939

Standing Figure, 1950

Helmet Head No. 2, 1950

If the position of any single element were changed the harmony of the whole would be destroyed. In one's imagination one can see a resemblance to the human figure stripped of all its non-essential references. The assembly is only 20 inches (51 cm) across. Yet if the scale were to be altered one could easily think of it as an architectural monument through which people could walk.

A carving that Moore made in 1936 must surely have a relationship to certain white relief compositions which Ben Nicholson began two years before. The stump-like base is sharply cut at an angle on the top to make a flat plane on which Moore has carved a geometrical arrangement of rectangles and circular indentations, as though one of Nicholson's paintings had been laid out on a table. This sculpture contains some of the only right angles to be found in any of Moore's work.

The sculptures discussed so far have all been carvings. *Three Points*, 1939 could not have been carved in stone or wood because these materials would have broken before its needle-sharp point had been finished. It was therefore cast in bronze from an original made in plaster. Moore himself links this work with details in some paintings. He refers to the outstretched fingers of God and Adam painted by Michelangelo in the Sistine Chapel. Though nothing is shown, one can almost feel the spark of life passing between them. The other reference is in a 16th-century painting of Gabrielle D'Estrées and her sister in the Louvre, where one woman's finger is poised to touch the nipple of her sister's breast. The sculpture reminds me of the electrodes in scientific apparatus across which the current leaps. The spiky shapes also have an association with the crown of thorns and the nails of the Crucifixion. Whatever the interpretation, the basic appeal of the sculpture is to our sense of touch and to our fear of sharp-pointed objects. It has a menacing beauty, and is one of Moore's most abstract works. These pointed images re-occur in his work at various stages in his life and are an example of his obsession with particular themes.

Other concepts may have originated from looking at three-dimensional models representing mathematical equations. Such sources also influenced the Constructivist artists. Naum Gabo was one such sculptor living in Hampstead during that period. Much of his work depends on the arrangement of strings threaded across an outer frame. Sculpture, which had for so long concerned itself with solidity and mass, was now being opened out to incorporate space as one of its basic elements. Moore's *Bird Basket* is a beautiful example of this kind of approach. Whether he envisaged the shape of a boat, a bird or a basket, is almost beside the point. The gracefulness and lightness of this sculpture is self-evident. There is no single point of view from which its quality is best appreciated. As one moves round it, its beauty is as continuous and as abstract as music.

The "biomorphic" principle is again seen at work in Moore's *Double Standing Figures* of 1950. Though he has since carved one of the figures in marble, the double image was conceived for casting in bronze. They have something of the air of warriors or sentinels with shields. Their bony skeletons, bound at knee and hip by powerful fleshy swellings, rise to strange split heads which look like eyes on stalks, warily on guard, and ready to seek the protection of the sharp triangular shields placed where the shoulder blades might be.

An artist who is interested in holes is also intrigued by caves, or for that matter, by helmets, skulls, shells and armour. Moore has made a number of sculptures dealing with this scheme and *Helmet Head No. 2*, 1950 is a forceful example. In this kind of sculpture there is always a contrast between the hard outer protective form and the more vulnerable object standing in the darkness within. This particular head has an air of watchful mystery.

Birth, war, procreation, all three are constant emotional feelings directly or indirectly present in much of Moore's sculpture. Procreation is the richest source of human experience to be related to shape and form. *Two Piece Interlocking*, as Moore dryly titles it, is one of his more tender interpretations of sexual love. It is carved out of one of the most inviting of all materials, white marble. It has always reminded me of polar bear cubs at play. Two separate pieces, each delightful in itself, are associated in a most complex arrangement of intertwined forms. Delicacy is marvellously balanced by inherent power. Moore abhors sweetness or sentimentality in art. In a context charged with sexual symbols, tenderness is the most difficult quality to achieve. When it is, power, beauty and feeling are united.

The abstract sculptures have always made it difficult for art critics to put Moore in his place. In Hampstead in the '30s, he was surrounded by

Two-piece Carving: Interlocking, 1968

all the temptations, turmoils and debates that heralded the arrival of modern art in Britain. Many were overwhelmed by the sheer weight of new ideas, and by modishly adopting one style or another they lost their own identity. Moore took from modern art what he wanted, and added it to what he had already assimilated from the past. He used nothing that did not serve his own purposes; his commitment to one movement or another was never wholehearted and complete.

André Breton, the leader of the French Surrealists, defined surrealism as "pure, psychic automatism. It is thought's dictation, all exercise of reason, and every aesthetic or moral preoccupation being absent". Moore had too acute an intelligence, as well as a sculptor's practical common sense, to agree. Too much psychological self-examination by an artist in pursuit of a scientific justification for his art can produce both bad art and bad science. Talking about drawing, Moore once said to me: "People think that artists are people who work for pleasure, by instinct, and without ever using their minds. There is a big intellectual effort in learning to draw properly. Leonardo showed it and Michelangelo showed it. They had great intellects. It is not a God-given gift to everybody that they can just draw!"

In Moore's view, art without thought is simply not worthwhile. "My real education," he has said, "was the British Museum—I did not get anything out of Hampstead—only friends." In Moore's opinion most of the arguments of the thirties contained truth, importance and necessity. All good art contained elements drawn from all of them. But single-minded crusades always left something out. Good art was simply the product of a good mind. Without that, you could do nothing. Writing in *The Listener* in 1937, he said:

> The conflict between the theories of surrealism and of pure abstraction leads many to look on one as black and bad, and the others as white and good. Yet it seems to me that a good work of art has always contained both abstract and surrealist elements—just as it has both Classical and Romantic elements (order and surprise?). Surrealism is widening the field of contemporary art and is giving more freedom to the artist (and what is not unimportant, stretching the appreciation of the public). Abstraction is re-

establishing fundamental laws, bringing back form to painting and sculpture ... there are many products of surrealism which I personally dislike—chaotic jumbles, paintings that are badly mixed salads of literary fantasy, pornographic shock stuff, echoes of the 1890s decadence. But equally unimportant to me are the empty decorations produced in the name of abstraction.

CHAPTER SIX
RECLINING FIGURES

Moore's earliest works were almost all modifications of a block being carved into a form that could be contained within it, such as the torso, the head, the Mother and Child, and standing figures cut off below the knee. Feet and legs are difficult to carve, since they carry the whole weight of the piece. It is easy for a standing figure to overbalance or break at the ankle. A reclining figure requires space that could scarcely be spared in the pieces of stone Moore could afford to buy. In the early days, if Moore as an artist wished to spread himself out, this was hardly possible. The problem could not, however, be postponed indefinitely. From about 1926, he began to concern himself with the full length female reclining figure. It has remained his central theme ever since. The formal advantages of turning the upright block on its side, in order to contain the elongated shape of the body, are numerous. For a sculptor the reclining position offers an endless series of possibilities, as legs and arms are changed, or as the spine or neck twists and turns in one direction or another. In a female figure the succession of shapes, openings, and swellings are full of sensuous beauty, no matter whether the sculptor considers his Eve to be the mother of man or a seductive temptress displaying her charms.

One of Moore's earliest surviving reclining figures was cast in concrete in 1927. She lies relaxed on a slab, like a contented cat, but her head is watchful. The shapes of this sculpture are already typically "Henry Moore". They are simple, smooth and compact. The effect is monumental. The whole piece is already suffused with his feeling for the landscape. The comparison between the human figure and the rolling slopes of hills or the worn-down shapes of boulders is inescapable. This blending of human and natural form, this ability to see figures in the landscape, and a landscape in the figures, is Moore's greatest contribution to sculpture. His works are literally landmarks.

The unexpected impact of Renaissance art, received from his visit to Italy in 1925, lay dormant for many years. A more immediate stimulus was the discovery of Mexican art. In particular, he had been deeply impressed by a copy of a Mexican rain spirit in the Trocadéro Museum in Paris, also in 1925. This massive sacrificial figure belonged to another civilization and another time, and was possibly 1,000 years old. Its religious significance was not Moore's concern. He saw in it a quality

Reclining Figure, 1929

that reminded him of the 11th-century carvings that he had seen in the Yorkshire churches during his childhood. Mexican sculpture seemed to him to be true and right. Its stoniness and its tremendous power suggested the ideal for which he was searching. He spoke of: "Its stillness and alertness, a sense of readiness—and the whole presence of it—the legs coming down like columns."

The first result of these perceptions was his seemingly massive reclining figure, carved in 1929 and now in the Leeds City Art Gallery. This figure has a more natural pose than its Mexican counterpart and the legs are turned to rest one upon another. One arm is raised to support the head, which is turned away from the body to look into the distance, with a slightly startled expression. Most important of all, the Mexican god has been turned into a generously proportioned earth-bound woman. Another related figure *Reclining Woman*, 1930 has her legs arranged in a more open posture, and her sexuality is further emphasized by the dynamic thrust of her mountainous breasts.

We are used to the idea that a painter's attraction to a subject is often

Reclining Figure, 1930
The first appearance of the 'hole'.

not the subject itself but, for example, its inherent qualities of light and colour. We are not so familiar with the concept of sculpture also being about qualities rather than subjects. Moore, like other sculptors, is interested in the nature of materials. Sea-worn pebbles reveal the wearing away and rubbed treatment of water, and the principles of asymmetry. Rocks have nervous, jagged rhythms as a result of being hacked, hewn and split. Bones offer immense variety of sections, making marvellous transitions between one shape and the next, within a single form. Their design is tense and gives evidence of immense structural strength, in spite of their lightness and their blade-like edges. Trees illustrate principles of growth and the strength of joints. Their upwards thrusting movements suggest ideal ways of working in wood. Shells, Moore notices, have a wonderful completeness of shape, with hard, hollow forms suitable for reproducing in metal. Stone, he argues, is hard and concentrated and should not be made to look like soft flesh, or forced beyond its natural strength to points of weakness. Some stones hold light, others reflect it. He asks us to see things for what they are. For example, to think of an egg not as food or something which will become a bird, but as a shape.

Moore began to explore the human figure in every possible way and in a wide variety of materials. Art, he believes, should have more meaning and mystery than is apparent to a quick observer. He says that he works from likes and dislikes, not from literary logic. Sculpture at first sight should have a degree of obscurity and further meaning. His first task was to open up the seemingly solid form of the human body in ways that exposed the expressive possibilities of human and natural correspon-dences. Like Wordsworth, he was to revitalize his chosen medium, by purifying its language, so as to directly express the elemental powers and moods of nature. One way to open up a sculpture is to dig a hole straight through it to the other side. Moore was not the first modern sculptor to do this. The credit for that perhaps belongs to the Russian-born sculptor, Alexander Archipenko, 20 years before. It had also been happening in paintings by Picasso and Braque, and in sculpture by Giacometti in the late '20s and early '30s. But it was left to Moore to develop this device in sculpture to greater effect than anyone else.

The small ironstone figure, only 8 inches (20 cm) long, that he carved in 1930, represents a first step, but the space made by its upraised arm

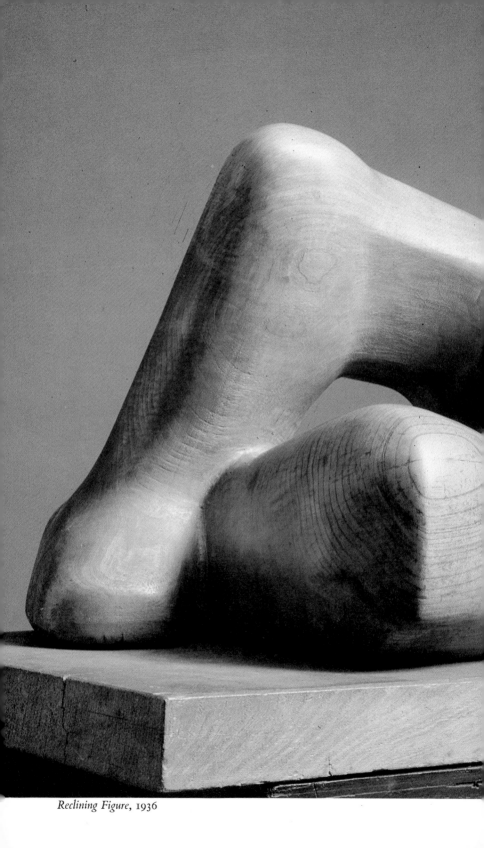

Reclining Figure, 1936

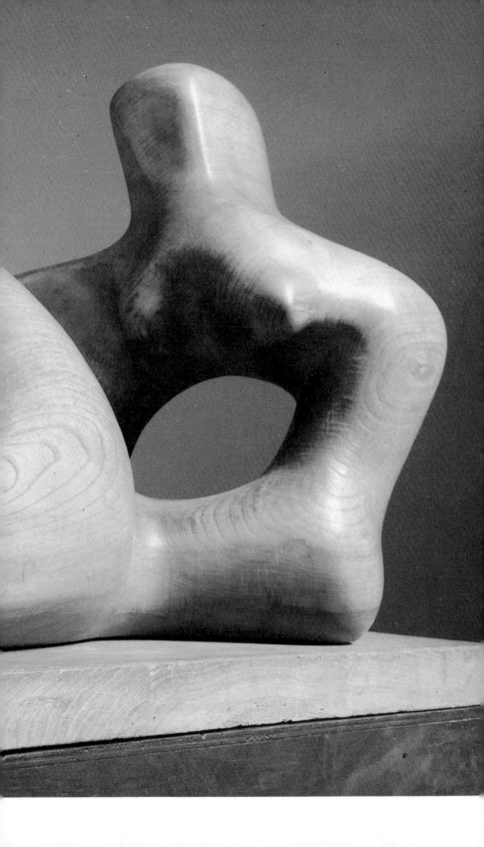

where it joins the head is still a natural space. However, by 1936, Moore's elm wood carving, now in the Wakefield Museum, shows how far he has developed a completely new system of sculptural expression. It seems larger than it really is, being 42 inches (107 cm) long. Its legs and torso form two quite separate units that flow smoothly into each other. By comparison with earlier works, there are remarkable changes within the volume of the figure. The cavity between its legs is repeated by a tunnel worn right through the chest. The breasts are suggested by protuberances on a great sheltering bridge, formed by the shoulders and the arms.

The whole process became far more intricate in Moore's later elm wood carvings, which grow in stature as the years go by until they become more than life-sized; his latest carving of this kind is as recent as 1978. The same ideas are also worked out in stone, in a variety of dignified yet massive sculptures that enlarge upon the flints and boulders that

fascinate Moore. Hollows, which anyone would admire if they came upon them in a landscape, become equally satisfying in the human context that Moore gives them. Space is as much a part of human sensibility as bulk. You cannot have one without the other, as anyone who walks into a cathedral apprehends. Enclosed space is the most effective space of all. Bodies are not made of solid rock. Flesh and bone are but the cover and support for the airs and fluids which flow through the inlets, cavities and tunnels by which we eat, live and breathe.

Moore's consideration of the human figure is not confined to these discoveries. The abstract and surrealist possibilities which inform so much of his other work also appear in some of the reclining figures, as in the mysteriously abstract *Reclining Figure*, 1937. To think in terms of wood or stone is one thing; metal is something else. The small *Lead Reclining Figure*, 1939 is 14 inches (35·5 cm) long. It would be impossible to carve it in stone or wood. Shapes such as these must be modelled on an armature

Reclining Figure: Curved, 1977

Draped Reclining Figure, 1952–53

in malleable materials, like plaster, wax or clay. Then a mould is made and cast in metal. Moore made some of these castings himself at home, in the kitchen, much to the alarm of his wife, who was proud of her pots and pans. This particular sculpture could almost be described as a metal drawing in space. Its contact with the ground is minimal. Its parts are as slim as served the sculptor's linear purpose. Nothing could be more smooth and liquid or so expressive of the elegant muscular articulation of the human form.

Moore was beginning to be as free and inventive in his sculpture as he already could be in his drawings. In the following year, a whole family of small metal figures produced an extraordinary range of fresh ideas. The spatial adventures are constantly surprising. Forms run into each other without interruption. There are suggestions of discs, struts, rods and straps. Breasts are quite literally wrapped about the body like a ring around a napkin, or hang on tense, stringy muscular supports.

In the two years before the war, one can sense an immense imaginative pressure building up as ideas proliferate. Since 1934, Moore had been renting a cottage in Kent, which had a large field. He could work in the open air with the added stimulus of sunlight and natural environment. The sea was not far away, and the cliffs and beaches were as exciting as the more restful landscape of the open downs.

Moore's sculpture is a remarkable display of non-mechanical engineering. It is the way of nature, not the way of the machine. His sculptures show us how the body feels rather than how it looks, and are the product of some mysterious inner sense of design. It is as if Moore's hands move and compose in reaction to some unconscious inner three-dimensional knowledge.

The war changed Moore's life in many ways. Some of the leading European artists went to America as refugees. His own move into the country meant that he saw less of his London friends. By now he was certain of his purpose and totally absorbed in his work. The need to take in new experiences was reduced. The economist, Maynard Keynes, had bought nine of his shelter drawings and a friendship developed that lead to Moore's appointment as a Trustee of the Tate Gallery, whose director was John Rothenstein, the son of Moore's former Rector of the Royal College. At the Tate he spoke up for the purchase of Degas' *Little Dancer*, and less successfully for the American sculptor, Alexander Calder.

Moore was beginning to be a public figure with friends in influential places. Amongst them he could count on Herbert Read, the art critic, Sir Philip Hendy, who was a director of the National Gallery, and Kenneth Clark (now Lord Clark), who held that position during the war. Another close friend was a leading literary figure, Geoffrey Grigson, and a frequent visitor to his Hertfordshire home was the art publisher, Peter Gregory. With such supporters it was not surprising that he undertook a wide range of public duties, serving as a Trustee of the National Gallery and as a member of the Royal Fine Art Commission, the National Theatre Board and the Arts Council of Great Britain. He was later to be elected a Fellow of the British Academy and the Royal Institute of British Architects, and an Honorary Member of the Royal Scottish Academy. As soon as the war was over, Moore began to carve again. In 1945 he made a mountainous elm wood figure whose somewhat helmet-shaped head has a face that is no more than a slit in a pill-box. This presides over a strange combination of thighs and hips that develop into a child's head, resting beneath the protective shield of its mother's chest.

He also carved a beautiful stone figure which was designed as a memorial to the founder of the Dartington Hall arts and education centre. It is one of Moore's most serene associations of figure and landscape. This sturdy figure is softened by graceful folds of drapery, which Moore had begun to use. In 1948, Moore won the International Prize for Sculpture at the Venice Biennale, and his work was in demand all over the world as further exhibitions spread his fame from country to country.

The 1951 *Reclining Figure* was commissioned for the Festival of Britain. It marks a development of the open forms that were used in his 1938 *Lead Figure*. This new figure was built up laboriously in plaster, and strings were applied to the surface to form fine lines that stand out in relief. The figure was cast in bronze, larger than life-size, and the contrast of the smooth shell-like forms with the slim bony supports gives parts of this sculpture an architectural feeling. This is particularly evident in the area where the torso is supported by firm but slender arches. The eye can pass through the sculpture from end to end without meeting any barrier.

In 1952 Moore returned to solid forms following a visit to Greece. The *Draped Reclining Figure* of that year is one of his most realistic works.

It was designed for a courtyard in the Time-Life building in London. In it he shows a completely new interest in the surface of his work. Details of it form a landscape of their own. A leg is clad in a cliff face of rippling textures. This leads to a body whose trunk is like an oak tree. The shoulder rises like a hill to a blunt head which is a lookout post on the summit. The lap is pitted like the surface of the moon. One of the practical problems that a sculptor has to consider for works intended to stand out of doors is to be certain that the rain can drain off the figure. In Italy, in the mountains behind Carrara, Moore was delighted to see rocks shaped and eroded by the elements in the same way; but the true origin of the figure must lie amongst the countless resting forms that he saw in the shelters during the war.

The famous marble quarries in the
Carrara Mountains, Italy.

Working model for *Reclining Figure*
(Lincoln Center), 1963-65

Moore's sculptural development progressed over the years from pre-occupations with the single figure towards the formal problems of balancing and relating separate parts of compositions that already had an individual identity. In 1959 he made a fundamental decision. The figure was to be taken apart and arranged as an assembly of quite separate pieces, often reminiscent of cliff faces and rock formations in the sea. He may have had in mind paintings by Seurat and Monet. It was also an obvious logical development of his own observation from nature, and his empathy for rocky and mountainous forms. Characteristically, Moore explains this splitting-up technique in purely practical terms.

Once a figure is in two pieces you don't expect it to be realistic, and therefore its relationship or analogy to landscape seems to be more natural. Again—with a single piece of sculpture, it is easier to guess what it is to be like from the other side; but when it is in two pieces, there are bigger surprises when you go round it, because one part will overlap another one and going round it becomes like a journey, as you have a different view all the time.

In the films that I have made with him, nothing has pleased Moore as much as seeing his sculptures revolving on turntables before the lens, or continuously revealing their perspectives as the camera glides past or moves into his work. The human figure is a starting-point for creating new forms. When Moore describes the work of the early Renaissance sculptor Giovanni Pisano, he points out how Pisano began to articulate the figure, showing the ability of its parts to move or thrust in different directions, gaining energy and vitality whilst retaining its static repose. The two-piece figure (1959) marks the beginning of what I would call Henry Moore's Bronze Age. Moore finds this medium ideal for expressing the forms of movement and thrust. By now he had become one of the most sought-after sculptors in the world, and this meant that he could develop his art free of economic considerations. It would be possible to plot on a graph a direct relationship between his income and the size of his work. The only limitations were the dimension of his studios, the weights that lorries could carry, and the ultimate restrictions of the bronze-casting process itself. There are only two foundries in Europe, one in England and one in Berlin, that can handle his largest projects.

Large Four-piece Reclining Figure,
1972–73

Moore was by now a master not only of form, but also of surface. He could command an enormous range of effect and mood. From work to work, the balance between realism and abstraction varies, as does the predominance of either landscape or the human figure. There are differences of emphasis between the contrasts of toughness and grace, between the rough and the smooth. One sculpture rises from out of water. Its torso is almost as sharp as a knife. It surges upwards with volcanic power. Some people find this sculpture, which was designed for the Lincoln Centre in New York, to be an expression of Moore's pessimism. I cannot see how this interpretation can be put upon it. To me it is a symbol of the indestructible powers of life, and pessimism seems utterly alien to any of Moore's creations and to his whole personality. In some of the divided figures, the pieces rest upon each other, as forms apart. Their points of contact generate a tension which takes us back to his earliest spiked forms or the stresses implicit in the structure of a bridge. No sooner has Moore pushed forward in one direction, than he turns in his tracks and goes off in an opposite way.

The Four Piece Reclining Figure, 1972-3 is one of the most abstract of his larger works. Its solid yet effortless shapes seem to add power even to the landscape where they stand. It is a work of great formal beauty and far more than just an assembly of characteristic parts.

Reclining Mother and Child, 1975-76

Reclining Woman, 1927 Cast in concrete by Moore himself.

Reclining Figure: Curved, 1977

The Reclining Mother and Child, 1975 displays a combination of opposites. The mother is a solid reality but the cradled child embodied in this realistic form is one of Moore's strange biomorphic abstractions, whose aggressive appetite seems remote from the mother's aloof calm. This is perhaps one work where the differently treated parts do not quite add up to a whole.

Other figures make use of forms found elsewhere in Moore's work, such as shells and stumps. Contrasting ideas lean up against each other almost in the way an anchor might be found lying against a harbour wall. Sometimes one is reminded of the vaguely human arrangements of masts, funnels, and ventilation cowlings on a ship's deck.

Fifty years have passed between the concrete figure of 1927 and Moore's black marble figure of 1977. Black materials are a new and mysterious element in Moore's sculpture, though they correspond to his use of darkness in drawings and prints. Far from denying form, Moore's highly polished surfaces, so coolly inviting to the touch, rest the eye without suggesting oblivion. The concrete woman he modelled in 1927 is full, rounded and youthful; ready to be aroused from her relaxation. The 1977 marble figure is more mature, and rests heavily on her arm. Both figures state their case with complete simplicity. The broad back of the black figure has immense strength beneath its powerful curve. The legs are drawn up and end in amputated points, but there is still unlimited power beneath the surface of the knee. Moore has never liked the waxen pallor and the leathery folds of Michelangelo's rendering of the flesh in his figure of "Night" in the sculpture of *Night and Day* on the tomb of the Medici in Florence. His own dark sculptures may have all the associations of approaching night and of sleep, but there is no slackness in the flesh. Their bodies have all the held-in power of a resting seal that may at any moment plunge into the ocean.

102

Madonna and Child, 1943

CHAPTER SEVEN
MONUMENTS FOR OUR TIME

The relationship between art and society is a fiercely debated issue about which Moore has said little. Some people feel that modern art in the 20th century has been wilfully elitist. It is also said that though our society encourages the training of artists, it has no idea what to do with them once they are trained. Moore himself rethought the meaning of sculpture in terms of his own sensibility and beliefs. He felt that the art of sculpture had lost its vitality but never doubted that an active culture was an inherent part of any form of society. However successful he may have been in satisfying his own needs, have his concerns resulted in works of art generally thought to be relevant to our time and accessible to the general public? Moore's drawings in the shelters and in the mines were about a common experience and did find a wide and appreciative public. What some commentators have overlooked is that Moore has continued to make a number of major sculptures, which are direct expressions of deeply felt experiences, common to people all over the world, during the post-war years. Such works whether they are privately or publicly

En route for the unveiling of the Northampton Madonna and Child.
(*l. to r.*) Graham Sutherland, Henry Moore, Myfanwy Piper.

owned have about them a generality of feeling and a relevance of subject matter that justifies calling them monuments.

The first such monument resulted from a specific request in 1943 to carve a Madonna and Child, surely the most traditional of subjects, for the church of St Matthew in Northampton. "I was not sure," Moore wrote at the time, "whether I could do it or whether I even wanted to do it. One knows that religion has been the inspiration of most of Europe's paintings and sculptures, but the great tradition of religious art seems to have got lost completely in the present day, and the general level of church art has fallen very low." He made numerous drawings and models to find out whether he could do something that satisfied him as an artist, and also satisfied his idea of what the theme suggested. The Mother and Child idea was not new to him. Moore began to ask himself how a Madonna and Child would differ, which was to ask himself in what way secular art differs from religious art.

It is not easy to describe in words what this difference is, except by saying in general terms that the 'Madonna and Child' should have an austerity and nobility, and some touch of grandeur (even hieratic aloofness) which is missing in the everyday 'Mother and Child' idea. Of sketches and models I have done, the one chosen had, I think, a quiet dignity and gentleness. I have tried to give a sense of complete easiness and repose as though the Madonna could stay in that position forever (as being in stone she will have to do).

Moore found a coherent and expressive style to fit the thought and the feeling implicit in his words. It is used in the *Reclining Figure* at Dartington Hall, and in the *Three Draped Standing Figures* in Battersea Park in London. These over life-size figures embody ideas already suggested by some of his wartime drawings. The women have come out of their shelters and stand warily in the open. They suggest a sense of relief felt by people after the war, who realized that they were still alive. They seem to look to the future with both apprehension and hope. It is a time for healing, for a return to the concerns of family and home. The quiet rhythms of these sturdy figures express perfectly the underlying mood in Britain in the years that followed the war. Nothing Moore has done has ever attained such effective simplicity.

Family Group, 1948-49

Three Standing Figures, 1947-48 (detail).

In 1946 his only child, Mary, was born. Two years later he began to work on a bronze *Family Group* that now stands in a public space in Stevenage new town. A somewhat similar stone carving was designed for Harlow, not far away. In spite of the complexities of the forms involved, he was again able to find a consistent style. It is realistic enough to be popular, yet powerful enough to give new life to a traditional idea. Both groups give a permanent expression to ideals that were very much a part of post-war Britain. The same ideas brought into being the welfare state with its emphasis on health, education and family security. It was the beginning of what politicians hopefully described as "the century of the common man"—and Moore's family groups gave a calm symbolic dignity to a humane aspiration.

Moore then found expression for another communal ideal. 1953 was the year of the Coronation of Elizabeth II. There was a great deal of popular excitement and much speculation about the nature of a new Elizabethan age. Moore's *King and Queen* can be seen as a deeply con- sidered statement about the nature and purpose of royalty. Technically this bronze shows evidence of his interest at that time in thin leaf and shell forms that could be modelled in wax. A visit to the site of Mycenae had given him a direct experience of Greek mythology. He must have seen 13th- to 15th-century B.C. figurines with strangely symbolic heads. The bird head, Moore reminds us, is a traditional symbol for royalty and the heads of his King and Queen incorporate the ideas of beard, crown and beak in a single form. The figures have an air of authority, but their grouping side by side emphasizes their domesticity. The real- istic modelling of their hands and feet illustrates their humanity. This Royal family serves as a multiple of parenthood and of the hieratic aspect of a couple who are also the symbolic parents of a nation, at one and the same time, stern, protective and remote.

Having said that, I must record that Moore now gives another account of how this group came into being. At the time his daughter was six years old and enjoyed being read to at bedtime. Inevitably many of the stories were about Kings and Queens. Moore had been experimenting with wax whilst modelling maquettes for his Madonna and Child and various family groups. He would press the soft wax into shapes between his fingers, and one of these dropped into a pan of hot water. It made a strange

shape that reminded him of a crown, so he made a head to go with it. That required a body, and then the whole figure demanded a Queen to go with it. He liked the thin, bent shapes that he could make out of strips of wax and used them for the bodies and the bench on which they sit. He denies that he had any conscious preconceived idea of making a "coronation" work. His account gives a happy illustration of the dangers of pressing too closely the relationships between artistic creation and social interpretation!

Falling Warrior. First stage of plaster in progress.

The *Falling Warrior*, 1956 again can be made to correspond to a development in public feeling. It represents a complete reversal of the Greek
ideal of martial virility and manhood. This man is no longer a hero. The
sculpture bears an aura of pathos. There was, at least in Western culture,
a profound revulsion against the military spirit and the futility of battle.
In England this general sense of disillusionment was forcefully expressed
in John Osborne's play *Look Back in Anger*. There were no proud causes
left worth dying for.

Falling Warrior. Finished plaster maquette ready for casting into bronze.

The finished *Falling Warrior*, 1956-57.

Reclining Figure, 1957-58
Carved by Moore himself on the site
of the UNESCO building in Paris.

In the same year, 1956, Moore was asked to provide a sculpture for the United Nations Education, Scientific and Cultural Organization, whose headquarters are in Paris. This at least was a direct social commitment. Picasso and Miró were also asked to provide work for the building. The commission highlights Moore's running battle with architects. The sculpture, on its own, is one of his most majestic achievements. The scale is awesome. Over 17 feet (5·2 m) long, it was carved from solid Roman Travertine marble. Moore first worked in the quarry outside Rome and then directly on the site in Paris. The form is of great simplicity and refers back in many ways to a much smaller figure carved in 1929, when he had been so directly inspired by the Mexican Chacmool rain spirit. What was needed was a symbol as explicit as Rodin's *The Thinker*. Moore's Earth Mother is appropriate as a symbol for the activities represented by UNESCO, an organization dedicated to the mothering of international co-operation in the arts and sciences. The only criticism is that it is a pity that architects always think of the embellishment of their buildings as an afterthought, instead of it being an essential part of their conception from the beginning.

Some monuments work on our imagination in less tangible and more primitive ways: the Ancient Celtic crosses on lonely moors, the huge stones at Avebury in Wiltshire, or the prehistoric sites in Brittany. Whether these are associated with magic, science or religion hardly matters. Moore has always had a side of his nature open to mysterious and magical impulses. The resulting biomorphic or archetypal shapes provoke indefinable responses in our feelings. Moore longed for a large scale expression of this. More than 60 such images had emerged during the 1960s, sometimes objects in the round, sometimes half-buried in reliefs. Some were eventually embodied in a sculptured brick wall in Rotterdam.

Three of these images were enlarged to stand 10 or 11 feet (3/3·3 m) high as sculptures in their own right. As a group, it was intended that they should be placed near a factory in Milan. Moore finally rejected the commission when he discovered that the site was to be in the middle of a car park. He has said about the sculptures that he likes their bony, bleached, fossil-like appearance, as though they were petrified trees. They are intended to be primitive and awe-inspiring. One of them, known in Britain

Upright Motive No. 1: Glenkiln Cross,
1955-56

as the Glenkiln Cross, was cast in an edition of seven, which stand in various parts of the world. This form reminds me strongly of Francis Bacon's paintings of tortured flesh, or the idea of the Crucifixion. Whether this thought was lurking in Moore's mind or not, the implications are there. The pedestal merges into the trunk, and the torso is arranged across this and topped with a seal-like Cyclops head. Images such as this defy rational explanation, but the work would be an appropriate, if unsentimental, memorial at any scene of human suffering or persecution. It is perhaps the responsibility of society, and not of the artist, to find relevance in such products of creation.

Atom Piece, 1964, on the other hand, is one of Moore's rare direct commissions to represent a specific theme, as was the case in the North-ampton Madonna. It is one of the very few sculptures by Moore which has its origins in a physical idea rather than in a natural form. The work belongs to the University of Chicago, where the Italian physicist Enrico Fermi made the first successful experiment in the controlled release of nuclear power. The symbolism therefore had to represent both physical and intellectual elements. The looming skull, with its highly polished surface, has the shape of the infamous mushroom cloud caused by the atomic bomb at Hiroshima. With its blank eye sockets, the head, in spite of its suave beauty, is a frightening evocation of death. It rises from a rocky base on cathedral-like columns, which give the interior an archi-tectural dimension. The smooth shape suggests the texture of a real mushroom, whose soft-rounded skin can split rocks as it grows upwards towards the light. This sculpture also relates to Moore's interest in the elephant skull given to him by his friend Julian Huxley, then Director General of UNESCO. Within the massive shapes of both sculpture and skull, one senses a high intelligence lurking in the shadows. Moore's ambiguous form acknowledges the intellect that sustains scientific dis-covery as well as the immensely powerful physical forces that are released, whether for good or for evil, just as fire can heat with its warmth or destroy with its flame. As an image for a nuclear age, this is a moral work which has no equal.

Many of these grand monumental images look at their best when set in landscapes. The *King and Queen* are superbly sited on a Scottish moor at Glenkiln, near Dumfries in Scotland. They can be seen against the back-

Atom Piece, 1964

ground of distant water and hills, or isolated against the sky. Indoors, Moore's sculptures make art galleries look like zoos, complete with their keepers to protect the spectators from the wild beasts. Moore has written that:

> Sculpture is an art of the open air. Daylight, sunlight, is necessary to it. And for me its best setting and complement is nature. I would rather have a piece of sculpture put in a landscape, almost any landscape, than in or on the most beautiful building I know. It was different in the Renaissance when a sculptor might be able to make his own architecture for his own sculptures. The idea that architecture is 'the mother of the arts' has put the sculptor into the position of being the architect's batman. The truth is that painting and sculpture existed long before architecture was even heard of.

It is not surprising therefore that in recent years Moore has made sculpture that becomes its own architecture, and makes its own environment. Some of his later works are big enough to walk through, as though they were tunnels, gorges or triumphal arches. One such arch, begun in 1963 and continued in various sizes and materials until 1969, is more than 15 feet (4·7 m) high; the largest bone in the world. When it was displayed at Moore's greatest retrospective exhibition in Florence in 1972, it became a popular landmark beneath which young bridal couples were photographed every day. This work demonstrates how much Moore's imaginative power has developed over the years. "Truth to Material" no longer matters if the shaped idea is strong enough to dominate any material in which it is rendered. Moore now says: "There is no such thing as truth to bronze—it can be anything."

The Arch, 1963-69
Full-scale model under construction, with working model alongside.

(*l.*) One of the finished versions; originally cast in fibreglass, later made in bronze.

Sheep Piece, 1971-72

Amongst these architectural pieces, I would pick out the *Large Two Forms* and *Square Form with Cut* as further examples of walk-through and walk-around sculptures that cunningly subvert fifty years of box-like rectangular architecture, which, at its worst, seems to be the ultimate in inhumanity. *Large Two Forms* is 15 feet (4·7 m) across. *Square Form with Cut* is 25 feet (7·6 m) high, and its 30 blocks of Carrara marble weigh 170 tons. The human desire for shape cannot be repressed forever. One has only to see the pleasure Moore's sculptures bring to those who touch them or walk through them to realize this. Children in particular climb over the surfaces and sit in the recesses and laps, watched by slightly embarrassed adults, who may be thinking that the children are experiencing a better physical relationship with the sculptures than they ever shared with their parents.

Sculptures of this size can cost as much as £100,000 to make. Few artists can afford to work on this massive scale. Fewer still could expand their ideas to meet the challenge. When Moore began, most of his work could be held in the hand or carved, gripped between his knees. Scale only works when one has got an idea to match. Sometimes, as in *Sheep Piece*, 1971, the statement is very direct and simple. At other times, as in *Three Piece Vertebrae*, 1968, it has prodigious sexual energy; or as in *Hill Arches*, 1973, an impressive structural vitality.

The last time I saw Moore's studio, he had just put aside an embryo model for a maze. In 1911, when Moore was still at school, the two sculptors, Jacob Epstein and Eric Gill, and the painter, Augustus John, were involved in an abortive attempt to build a secret "Temple of 100 Pillars". It was to be a 20th-century Stonehenge, standing in the English countryside. Could something similar still happen?

CHAPTER EIGHT
LOOKING BACK

Looking back on his life, Moore has few complaints. He does, I think, feel that life is sometimes made too easy for a younger generation of artists. He has a strong, puritan belief in the values of work, learning and effort. He recalls that between the two World Wars, few artists in England made any money from their work. Epstein and Augustus John are two who come to mind. Most of his contemporaries, Paul Nash, Barbara Hepworth, Ben Nicholson, Matthew Smith, and his ardent supporter, William Rothenstein, had some private income or could be helped by their parents. Moore had to make his own way unaided. Until he was 50, he was earning about as much as an average school teacher. The breakthrough came after he won the international prize for sculpture at the Venice Biennale in 1948. That made him an international figure. Very few British artists had then achieved that status in the 20th century. It was a German art dealer, Curt Valentin, who introduced his work to the United States. Moore acknowledges a considerable debt to Germany, Italy and America. Even now, more than three-quarters of his work is sold abroad, mostly to the United States.

When he started, Moore felt that he was almost alone in England and that the art of sculpture had been dormant since the Middle Ages. This of course is to ignore a mass of 18th- and 19th-century academic work which was to him of no interest. Artists such as Picasso, Brancusi, Archipenko, and the Surrealists had established new freedoms. It was suddenly possible to see art in terms of world-wide tradition, with its origins going back 40,000 years in history. Moore says that it was like being born at the beginning of a new Renaissance. At that time in England Moore and Barbara Hepworth, his colleague at Leeds and the Royal College, stood almost alone. Since the war, most of the European leaders of the modern movement have come to pay their respect to their English comrade. Brancusi emerged from retirement from his studio in Paris to shake hands with a fellow master. Miró, Braque, Ernst, Léger and Le Corbusier, all visited Moore in his studio. The Italian sculptor Marino Marini became one of his closest friends.

Moore usually goes to Italy every summer, and lives in a pleasant villa near Viareggio. He spends the morning on the beach, outside a bathing-hut which is just like all the others that stretch for miles along this coast. With his wife and family, he is indistinguishable from the other holidaymakers relaxing in the sun. Only the Italian woman who owns the cabin he uses knows the difference. "Ah," she says, "Henry Moore—Michelangelo—" and presses her knuckles against her forehead in an eloquent gesture.

The amazing stockyard belonging to the Henraux Marble Company is nearby. In their sheds, machines cut, grind and polish stone from all over the world. In studios provided by the company, Italian masons with paper caps on their heads to protect them from the dust, work on forms envisaged by many of the world's greatest sculptors. Moore will run his finger over a surface, detecting lumps and imperfections, all but invisible to the eye.

Beyond, high in the mountains, lies a quarry once owned by the Medici, where Michelangelo found stone for his statue of "David". On the highest peak, men with wires, drills and explosives slice into the mountain, just as has been done for centuries. Far below, lorries crawl down slopes like ants, bearing blocks of the purest white marble. Each block is as big as a room in a fair-sized house. Moore is very happy showing his friends around this place, and deeply moved by the mountain ranges on every side. "Sculpture is the energy of mountains," he recalls. He has come a long way from the broad expanses of the Yorkshire moors. This Italian prospect is more majestic and imbued with all the potency of a long cultural tradition.

Yet Henry Moore remains completely an Englishman at home in his own country. His roots will never permit him to leave his native soil for long. In the calm of his Hertfordshire setting, where he has lived for 40 years or so, the routine is much as it ever was—breakfast, the 9 o'clock briefing of his staff for the day ahead, the consultation with his secretary as she deals with the correspondence and re-arranges his diary yet again. Then comes a round of the studios before the visitors arrive.

As the day's guests come, Moore deals with the museum and gallery representatives, the collectors, the publishers, the journalists and photographers, and the various printers and craftsmen who collaborate in his enterprises. With luck, there might be an hour to spare to do some drawing before the 1 o'clock lunch. In the afternoon, there may be another round of duties. More visitors, more obligations; or he might have to go to London to attend to business there. At 80, he even flies to Berlin and

Putting the finishing touches to part of *Square Form with Cut*, 1969-72, in the stoneyards near Carrara.

back in a day. Miraculously, somewhere, somehow, in the 24 hours of such days, he manages to get lost to the world and continue his unabated flow of work.

Even after the world-wide celebrations of his 80th birthday the incessant activity continues. There was to be an exhibition in Madrid and another the following year in Mexico. A huge reclining figure had been shipped to the Empress of Iran. It arrived at Teheran during the revolution, and nothing further had been heard of it. It had been paid for. The village complex hums with activity and has something of the atmosphere of a shipyard, a publishing house, and an education centre combined. Wherever you go around the studios the eye is confused by a litter of brushes, cheese-graters, rasps, spoons, knives, mallets, hammers, chisels, files, saws, pliers, sponges, spatulas, scissors, pencils, pens, jars, pans, paints, varnishes, punches, points and claws, lying amongst piles of papers, boxes, bags of plaster, and half-formed slabs of polystyrene.

Moore's most treasured possession is his Cézanne oil sketch. At the suggestion of his friend Stephen Spender, he copied three of the figures and modelled them in clay, and then in plaster to show that Cézanne's grasp of form was so good that the unseen view of the figures would be as effective as the backs he had painted, and that what worked in two dimensions could equally well be translated into three. It is a strange experience to step inside Cézanne's little painting and see it from the other side. I asked Moore about his maze. He corrected me and said that it was really a model for a kind of Stonehenge—a temple or an enclosed space through which people could move without seeing outside. He doubted if it would ever be done, especially as he had really imagined it as an underground sculpture—like a series of caves or pot-holes. He recalled playing in his childhood in a place near home called "Sandbanks". Children would crawl into a warren of tunnels, with a reel of cotton to find their way back. The idea would take ten years to do, he said sadly, though someone was coming the next day to talk to him about it. It was a poignant reminder of weeks spent in the underground shelters and down the mine at Castleford during the war.

Time will show that Moore and Picasso have been the two greatest figures in modern art, whatever the rest of this century may bring. There is an essential difference between the two. Picasso was the man who

Henry Moore's Cézanne painting
Trois Baigneuses, with his
interpretation of it in bronze (1979).

let all the sheep out of the pen to run loose through the landscape. Moore is the shepherd who rounded up the flock and directed them back towards their traditional pastures. He talks of Rembrandt, Cézanne, Rodin and Michelangelo as though they were still alive and members of the same family, or at least intimate colleagues living with him in the present.

Moore has restated a belief that the human figure is the beginning and the end of art, and that art itself is a vision of life. He liberated sculpture from a narrow set of rules that was stifling its development. He restored vitality to form and showed that sculpture could be used with a freedom and a range of self-expression that painters had already won for themselves. He showed how the human figure felt, as well as how it looked. He merged its forms with those of the rest of the natural world about it. He introduced space into a solid art and made a tangible reality of images hidden in the mind. After Moore, sculpture can never again be only a kind of pictorial painting in three dimensions. His approach to progress is evolutionary, not revolutionary. He has not equated art with science nor with social propaganda, technology or pseudo-psychology. He has avoided the politics of art and the military tactics of some of its supporters. He would prefer to see himself as an artist who has tried to forge a new link in a chain. His English temperament has avoided extremes. He has preferred to seek a point of equilibrium, of balance between the opposing forces in art, in life, and in nature.

In the atmosphere of peace that pervades his studios, and the country-side around, it is hard to believe that so much has happened there. There is as yet little evidence of other sculptors realizing this either. Succeeding generations of younger men inevitably set out, as Moore did himself, to establish their own originality.

At times the 20th century has seemed a dispiriting period for the survival of civilized values and for individual genius. In such moods a visit to Henry Moore's studios gives one a heartening sense of reassurance. Human life and endeavour seem indestructible, after all.

Plaster model of a stone maze
intended either as a hill sculpture or an
underground project.

BIBLIOGRAPHY

The most complete general survey of Henry Moore's work is contained in the four volumes published by Lund Humphries between 1944 and 1977: **Henry Moore, Sculpture and Drawings.** Vol. 1 is edited by David Sylvester; Vol. 2 has an introduction by Herbert Read; and Vols. 3 and 4 are edited by Alan Bowness.

The most readily available general studies in English are:

Henry Moore by Herbert Read (Thames & Hudson, 1965)
Henry Moore by John Russell (Allan Lane The Penguin Press, 1968; with revision in Pelican Books, 1973)
Henry Moore, Sculpture and Drawings edited by Robert Melville (Thames & Hudson, 1970)

Two essential books for the study of Moore's drawings are:

Henry Moore: Unpublished Drawings by David Mitchinson (Fratelli Pozzo, Turin, 1974)
Henry Moore, Drawings by Kenneth Clark (Thames & Hudson, 1974)

Photographic surveys of the artist and his studios:

Henry Moore photographed by John Hedgecoe (Nelson, 1968)
With Henry Moore photographed by Gemma Levine (Sidgwick and Jackson, 1978)
Henry Moore, Sculptures in Landscape photographed by Geoffrey Shakerley (Studio Vista, 1978)

The most complete collection of statements by the artist is:

Henry Moore on Sculpture edited by Philip James (MacDonald, 1966)

1898 Henry Moore born 30 July at Castleford, Yorkshire, the seventh child of Raymond Spencer Moore (1849-1921) and Mary Baker (1860-1944).

1910 Wins a scholarship to Castleford Grammar School. Encouraged in art by his teacher, Miss Gostick, and introduced to Gothic sculpture and local church architecture by the headmaster, J. R. Dawes.

1915-16 Becomes a student teacher on the wishes of his father, and takes up teaching post at his old elementary school in Castleford.

1917 Moore's first visit to London. Discovers the British Museum and the National Gallery. Joins the 15th London Regiment in February and is sent to the Front at the beginning of summer. Gassed at the Battle of Cambrai and returns to England in December.

1919 Army discharge pension allows him to give up teaching post and enrol at the Leeds School of Art for two years.

1921 Wins scholarship to the Royal College of Art in London. Makes frequent visits to the British Museum and sees Egyptian, Etruscan and Mexican sculpture.

1922 Moore spends vacation in Norfolk, where he starts doing sculpture out of doors. Makes his first direct carvings in stone and wood—influenced by primitive and archaic sculpture, and by Gaudier Brzeska and Epstein.

1923-24 First of many annual visits to Paris, where he sees the Cézannes in the Pellerin Collection. Gains his Diploma at the Royal College of Art and becomes Professor of Sculpture there.

1925 Awarded Royal College of Art travelling scholarship and spends six months in France and Italy. Studies Michalangelo, Giotto, and Masaccio.

1928 First one-man exhibition at the Warren Gallery, London. Moore receives his first public commission—a relief carving for St. James's Park underground station.

1929 Moore marries Irina Radetzky, a painting student at the Royal College, and moves into a studio at 11a Parkhill Road, Hampstead. First reclining figure influenced by the Mexican Chacmool sculpture. First appearance of the 'hole' in his work. Begins collecting pebbles, shells and bones.

1931 One-man show at the Leicester Galleries, London, with an introduction by Epstein. First abstract forms.

1932 Appointed Head of new sculpture department at Chelsea School of Art.

1933 Joins 'Unit One', founded by Paul Nash. Collaborates on the magazine *The Group* edited by Herbert Read.

1934 Moves to larger studio at Kingston, near Canterbury, in Kent. Publication of Herbert Read's monograph: *Henry Moore, Sculptor*.

1936 Visits Spain, including a tour of the Altamira cave paintings. Signs the manifesto against non-intervention in Spain, and exhibits at the International Surrealist Exhibition in London.

1937 First stringed figures in wood. Moore starts to use maquettes, rather than carving directly on the basis of a drawing.

1939 He gives up teaching, and makes the first helmet heads; a series he continues after the war.

1940 Moore returns to London. His studio in Hampstead is partly demolished during the Blitz, and he moves to Perry Green, Much Hadham—where he still lives. Produces first shelter drawings as an official War Artist.

1941 First retrospective exhibition at Leeds. Becomes a trustee of the Tate Gallery.

1942 Returns to Castleford as a War Artist to draw miners at the coal face.

1943 First one-man exhibition abroad at the Buchholz Gallery, New York (drawings). Commissioned to carve a Madonna and Child for the Church of St. Matthew, Northampton.

1944 Works in plaster and wax. First bronzes. Maquettes on the theme of the Family Group. Moore is created Honorary Doctor of Literature at Leeds University—his first academic award.

1945 Moore goes to Paris to meet Brancusi.

1946 Birth of daughter Mary. First visit to the United States with a retrospective exhibition at the Museum of Modern Art, New York.

1948 Moore wins the International Sculpture Prize at the 24th Venice Biennale. Returns to Italy for the first time since 1925.

1949 Begins doing draped figures. Retrospective exhibition at Musée d'Art Moderne in Paris.

1950 Works on Arts Council commission for a large bronze reclining figure for the 1951 Festival of Britain.

1951 First visit to Greece. Retrospective exhibition at the Tate Gallery, London. First film about Moore's work for BBC-TV, directed by John Read.

1952 Moore begins work on the *King and Queen*, and accepts project for the Time-Life building in London.

1953 Visits Mexico and Brazil and receives the International Sculpture Prize at Sao Paulo.

1955 Moore made Companion of Honour and trustee of the National Gallery.

1956-57 Commissioned to make a sculpture for the UNESCO headquarters in Paris. Receives the Carnegie International Prize in Pittsburgh.

1959 Starts to divide the reclining figure into separate parts. Receives the International Prize for Sculpture in Tokyo.

1963 Awarded the Order of Merit. *Two Piece Reclining Figure* commissioned for the Lincoln Center, New York.

1964 Buys a cottage at Forte dei Marmi in Italy, near the Carrara quarries, as a summer studio for stone carving.

1966 Begins the *Atom Piece* for a monument to Enrico Fermi in Chicago. *The Archer* is erected in front of City Hall, Toronto. Start of renewed interest in graphics.

1968 Moore's 70th Birthday is marked by major exhibitions at the Tate Gallery and elsewhere in Europe.

Awarded the Erasmus Prize, and gives part of the proceeds to the St. Katherine's Dock scheme to help young artists.

1972 Major exhibition at the Forte di Belvedere in Florence.

1974 Opening of the Henry Moore Sculpture Centre at the National Gallery of Ontario, Toronto.

1977 Exhibition in Paris at the Orangerie des Tuileries.

1978 8oth Birthday. Makes gift of 36 sculptures to the Tate Gallery. Exhibitions held there and elsewhere in London, and in Bradford and Tokyo. BBC TV film *Henry Moore at 80* is shown throughout the world.

1979 Sculptures based on Cézanne's painting of bathers are finished. The Henry Moore Foundation building, next door to his home in Perry Green, is opened.

LIST OF ILLUSTRATIONS

49 *Head of an Old Man,* 1921
Pencil. 6 × 6¼ in (*15·2 × 15·8 cm*).
Art Gallery of Ontario.

50 *Seated Woman,* 1921
Pencil, pen and ink, wash.
12 × 9 in (*30·5 × 22·9 cm*).
Trustees of the British Museum.

53 *Standing Figure,* 1923
Pencil, pen and ink, wash.
11⅝ × 6⅞ in (*29·5 × 17·5 cm*).

54 *Standing Nude,* 1926
Pencil, pen and ink, chalk, and wash.
17¼ × 8¼ in (*43·8 × 21 cm*).

55 *Standing Nude,* 1927
Pen and wash.
14½ × 9¼ in (*36·8 × 23·5 cm*).

57 *Seated Figures,* 1931
Pen and ink, chalk, wash.
14⅝ × 10¾ in (*37·2 × 27·3 cm*).

58 People sheltering in the London
Underground during the Blitz.

59 *Two Sleepers,* 1941
Chalk, wax crayon, watercolour.
12 × 18 in (*30·5 × 45·7 cm*).

61 Henry Moore down the mine at
Castleford, 1942. Henry Moore.

62 *Miners' Faces,* 1942
Pen and ink, wax crayon, wash.
9⅞ × 7 in (*25·1 × 17·8 cm*).

63 *Figures with Architecture,* 1943
Pen and ink, black and coloured
chalks, wax crayon, wash.
17½ × 25 in (*44·5 × 63·5 cm*).

65 *Shipwreck,* 1973
Pencil, charcoal, ballpoint pen, wash.
7½ × 6⅞ in (*19 × 17·5 cm*).

66 *Sheep Sketchbook,* 1972
Ballpoint pen.
8¼ × 9⅞ in (*21 × 25 cm*).

67 *Trees Drawing IV,* 1975
Charcoal and wash on blotting paper.
11⅝ × 7⅞ in (*29·5 × 20 cm*).

68 *'Gus'*
Page 3 from White Notebook, 1978.
Pencil. 11½ × 7⅞ in (*29 × 20 cm*).

70 *Composition,* 1931
Green Hornton stone.
H. 19 in (*48·3 cm*).

74 *Three Points,* 1939-40
Cast iron. L. 7½ in (*19·1 cm*).

74 *Bird Basket,* 1939
Lignum vitæ and string.
L. 16½ in (*41·9 cm*).

75 *Standing Figure,* 1950
Bronze. H. 87 in (*221 cm*).
Edition of 4.

75 *Helmet Head No. 2,* 1950
Bronze, H. 14 in (*35·6 cm*).
Edition of 9.

78 *Two-piece Carving: Interlocking,* 1968
White marble. L. 28 in (*71 cm*).

83 *Reclining Figure,* 1929
Brown Hornton stone.
L. 33 in (*83·8 cm*).
City Art Gallery and Museum, Leeds.

84 *Reclining Figure,* 1930
Bronze. L. 7 in (*17·8 cm*). Edition of 2.

86 *Reclining Figure,* 1936
Elmwood. L. 42 in (*106·7 cm*).
City Art Gallery, Wakefield.

88 *Reclining Figure,* 1938
Lead. L. 14 in (*35·6 cm*).
Museum of Modern Art, New York.

90 *Draped Reclining Figure,* 1952-53
Bronze. L. 62 in (*157·5 cm*).
Edition of 3 (on exhibition at Ely
Cathedral, 1973).

94 The famous marble quarries in the
Carrara Mountains, Italy.

95 *Working Model for Reclining Figure,*
(Lincoln Center), 1963-65
Bronze. L. 14 ft (*4·27 m*). Edition of 2.

96 *Large Four Piece Reclining Figure,*
1972-73
Bronze. L. 13 ft 2 in (*4·03 m*).
Edition of 7.

98 *Reclining Mother and Child,* 1975-76
Bronze. L. 84 in (*213·4 cm*).
Edition of 7.

100 *Reclining Woman,* 1927
Cast concrete. L. 25 in (*63·5 cm*).

101 *Reclining Figure: Curved,* 1977
Black marble. L. 56½ in (*143·5 cm*).

103 *Madonna and Child,* 1943
Hornton stone. H. 59 in (*149·9 cm*).
Church of St. Matthew, Northampton.

104 Graham Sutherland, Henry Moore,
Myfanwy Piper. Henry Moore.

106 *Family Group,* 1948-49
Bronze. H. 60 in (*152·4 cm*).
Edition of 4.

108 *Three Standing Figures,* 1947-48
(detail)
Darley Dale stone. H. 84 in (*213 cm*).
Battersea Park, London.

111 *King and Queen,* 1952
Bronze. H. 64½ in (*164 cm*).
Edition of 5.

112 *Fallen Warrior,* 1956
Finished plaster maquette ready for
casting into bronze. H. 9 in (*22·9 cm*).

113 *Falling Warrior,* 1956
First stage of plaster in progress.

114 *Falling Warrior,* 1956-57
Bronze. L. 58 in (*147·32 cm*).
Edition of 10.

115 *Reclining Figure,* 1957-58
Roman Travertine marble.
L. 16 ft 8 in (*5·09 m*).
UNESCO Building, Paris.

117 *Upright Motive No. 1: Glenkiln
Cross,* 1955-56
Bronze. H. 11 ft (*3·36 m*).
Edition of 6.

119 *Atom Piece,* 1964
Bronze. H. 48 in (*122 cm*).
Edition of 6.

120 *The Arch,* 1963-69
Full-scale version cast in fibreglass.
Bronze version made later.
H. 20 ft approx. (*6·1 m*).

122 *Sheep Piece,* 1971-72
Bronze. H. 18 ft approx. (*5·5 m*).
Edition of 3. Photo: Philip Sayer.

127 *Square Form with Cut,* 1969-72
White marble.
Completed height 17 ft 10 in (*5·45 m*).
Now in situ, City of Prato, Italy.

129 *Trois Baigneuses,* 1873-77,
by Paul Cézanne. Oil on canvas.
12 × 13 in (*30·5 × 33 cm*).

129 *Three Bathers—After Cézanne,* 1978
Henry Moore's interpretation in
bronze.
L. 12 in (*30·5 cm*). Edition of 3.

131 Plaster model of a stone maze
intended either as a hill sculpture or a
underground project.

Endpapers. From a Henry Moore
sketchbook, 1926.

Front Cover Henry Moore. Photo:
Philip Sayer.

Back Cover Sheep Sketchbook, 1972.
Sheep Piece, 1971-72. Photo: Philip Sayer.

Photographs of all drawings and sculptures courtesy of Henry Moore.

INDEX